D1021746

The Early Care and Education Teaching Workforce at the Fulcrum

AN AGENDA FOR REFORM

Sharon Lynn Kagan
Kristie Kauerz
Kate Tarrant

Teachers College, Columbia University
New York and London

Published by Teachers College Press, 1234 Amsterdam Avenue, New York, NY 10027

Library of Congress Cataloging-in-Publication Data

Kagan, Sharon Lynn.
  The early care and education teaching workforce at the fulcrum : an agenda for reform / Sharon Lynn Kagan, Kristie Kauerz, Kate Tarrant.
    p. cm. — (Early childhood education series)
  Includes bibliographical references and index.
  ISBN 978-0-8077-4827-5 (pbk. : alk. paper)
  1. Early childhood teachers—United States. 2. Early childhood education—United States. 3. Child care—United States. I. Kauerz, Kristie. II. Tarrant, Kate. III. Title.

  LB1775.6.K34 2008
  372.11—dc22

                                                              2007016906

ISBN: 978-0-8077-4827-5 (paper)

Printed on acid-free paper
Manufactured in the United States of America

15 14 13 12 11 10 09 08   8 7 6 5 4 3 2 1

To the scores of wonderful individuals
who work with young children daily,
whose commitment and efforts do nothing less
than shape the future
and
Julius Richmond,
master shaper of our nation,
who taught us so much about children,
their families, and social change

Contents

Preface

> Fulcrum: the support about which a lever turns; one that supplies capability for action; a part . . . that serves as the hinge or support.
> —*Merriam-Webster's Collegiate Dictionary*

IT HAS LONG been noted that the quality of any institution—be it a Fortune 500 corporation, a world-renowned university, or a nonprofit organization—hinges on one factor: the quality of its workforce. Indeed, a quality workforce is the fulcrum around which every institutional achievement pivots. Business and industry magnates the world over have known this for decades and have taken steps to ensure a quality workforce. In contrast, early care and education (ECE), broadly defined as the services that support the development and education of children birth to age 5, has been less well-resourced and hence less able to address the needs of its workers, especially its teachers, despite the fact that those who work directly with young children are at the fulcrum of the lives of the children and families they serve. The ECE teaching workforce enables children to learn, families to work, and the American economy to thrive. But the fulcrum is precarious; the ECE teaching workforce, while having the capability for action, is stymied; it lacks the opportunities it enables for others. This book is about that workforce. It paints the portrait of teachers who deserve support commensurate with that which they provide.

As a field characterized by low entry criteria, limited growth opportunities, low compensation, and high turnover, ECE today faces severe workforce challenges. Paradoxically, investments in early care and education are at an all-time high, as are fiscal commitments from policymakers at local, state, and federal levels. More and more children are enrolled in ECE programs, many from families who rely on these programs to enable them to go to work each day, many from families who choose to have their children in settings that will nurture and enrich the children's learning experiences. But, with the expansion of early care and education, awareness of workforce challenges also is expanding, fueling the desire to address historic and deep-seated challenges in new ways. Indeed, there presently are building blocks that can guide the field: a burgeoning research base, coupled with scores of innovative and significant workforce improvement efforts. There is also a successful model of social change that can be used to guide future efforts. Advanced by Julius Richmond—scholar, physician, and social advocate—to whom this book is dedicated, the model specifies three conditions that are necessary for social reform: a well-codified knowledge base, political and public will, and a social strategy. We adopt Richmond's triad as the conceptual and organizational frame for this volume, which is devoted to significantly strengthening the ECE fulcrum, its teaching workforce.

This book aims to provide a single, consolidated resource that synthesizes what is known about the ECE teaching workforce: It addresses the issues comprehensively—across all segments of the ECE field, and across a range of workforce improvement strategies. It incorporates information on the early care and education workforce in all forms of center- and home-based services, highlighting a large number of workforce improvement efforts. In addition to being comprehensive, the book also seeks to be highly methodical; it provides a framework to both conceptualize and categorize contemporary workforce efforts. This framework, then, facilitates an analysis of the range of research and field-based efforts underway, pinpointing areas where the field is excelling and areas where more effort is needed. Specifically, the volume provides information regarding: (a) the status of the American early care and education teaching workforce, (b) the quality and effectiveness of this workforce, and (c) a compendium of current strategies being used to improve it. Combining comprehensive research and field-based data with a fresh analytical framework, we also render a set of recommendations that offer a new way to think about a system of workforce enhancement. Intended to be reflective and forthright, the book does not mince words; while commending actions that have taken place to date, it suggests that a more comprehensive, equitable, and systemic approach is needed.

In the course of writing this volume, we faced several critical challenges. Some of these were predictable: large holes in the available research data, insufficient information regarding many of the truly "lighthouse" practice efforts, and redundancy in the recommendations historically proffered. One major challenge, while also predictable, was of such transcendent importance that we wrestled with it daily. The lack of definitional clarity has characterized the field for decades, with numerous debates regarding what to call this important work: early education, early childhood education, early care and education, preschool. While it may be confusing, we have elected to use the term *early care and education (ECE)* because it is a term that embraces many different types of programs serving young children. Even more problematic, however, is the field's inconsistent use of terms immediately germane to the content of this book: teachers, workforce, turnover, professional development, education, and training. Finally, in our review of research, we found that many studies address different segments of the early care and education workforce (e.g., Head Start or child care or prekindergarten), making it very difficult to portray the workforce—across all programs, program types, and states—as a whole. To standardize our analysis, we developed and adopted a set of definitional terms that are used throughout this book. Many of our definitions are embedded throughout the content of the book, with the central ones presented in Chapter 1.

This work owes its existence to numerous individuals. With both intellectual and financial support from Cornerstones for Kids and Ira Cutler, we were able to think comprehensively and deeply about the early care and education workforce both independently and within the broader human services workforce context. An Advisory Committee, composed of stellar scholars and thinkers, guided us regarding the studies and projects to be reviewed and advanced our thinking about the data and the recommendations. We thank them all—Nancy Folbre, Carollee Howes, Sue Russell, Louise Stoney, Marcy Whitebook, Dan Bellm, Marci Young, and Martha Zaslow. We also thank the numerous individuals from states and specific workforce initiatives who shared with us their time, knowledge, wisdom, and data. Despite this input, we alone bear the burden of errors, omissions, and misinterpretations. The "we" in this case includes, in addition to the authors, Amy Berliner Carson, who worked with us diligently on the report on which this volume is based. She lent her considerable research, writing, and analytical talents to the study. Erica Greenberg contributed mightily to this volume, rendering tireless conceptual and editorial expertise. We wish to warmly acknowledge Carole Saltz, whose insights and commitment are legion; we are lucky to have her as our editor and colleague. We also wish to acknowledge Teachers College Press, which has provided years of support to advance the field of early care and education in America and worldwide.

To these people—and to the countless teachers, children, and dedicated ECE professionals who have touched and shaped each of us over the years—we offer our deepest gratitude.

The ECE Teaching Workforce: Today and Tomorrow

Today's Workforce Matters

TRUE STORY 1: THE TEACHERS' PERSPECTIVE

Emma Williams has worked as a lead teacher in a child care center for 7 years. A single mother of three children, she relies on her job to support her family. She wanted to be an early care and education teacher because she loves children and thought the experience would improve her parenting. Today, Emma Williams left her child care center with mixed emotions. Sad to leave the children and her colleagues, she is overjoyed at earning twice as much money (not including retirement benefits and health benefits for herself and her children), at having a 10-month work year, and at having less responsibility as a teacher's assistant in the new prekindergarten down the block.

TRUE STORY 2: THE PARENTS' PERSPECTIVE

Lucinda and George Stiles are the working parents of three preschool-aged children. Earning a solid income and having some job flexibility, they want top-notch early care and education for their youngsters but are not quite sure exactly what to look for. On the surface, they seem to be lucky; they live in a community with a state-funded pre-kindergarten for 4-year-olds and many child care centers. Because of their own work schedules and logistics, they would like to keep the children together in one early care and education program, but they decide to put their eldest, the 4-year-old, in the half-day prekindergarten program for the mornings. They search for child care for the other two children only to find that the center they think is good is already filled. Disappointed, they waitlist the two children at the center and, in the meantime, to solve their family child care crisis, put the children in a family child care home. Here, their prekindergartener can join his two siblings during the afternoon. The Stiles adore their family child care provider and think she is good, but she has just put them on notice that she is giving up her work to pursue a real estate broker's license.

TRUE STORY 3: THE POLICYMAKERS' PERSPECTIVE

In Emmetsburg, Anystate, Speaker of the State House of Representatives Mike Forest just attended a conference on early care and education. He went to the conference because several local businesspeople had complained: It wasn't just that their work-force wasn't well educated enough, it was that they couldn't keep female workers who had young children. Mike thought some kind of policy might address both is-sues. At the conference, he learned about brain research, the importance of the early years, and the demonstrated success of many early care and education programs around the country. But Mike also heard about legions of quality and "pipeline" problems. He was perplexed: How could he use legislation to help get better teachers into these programs to boost program quality, without making costs so exorbitant that his fellow representatives would vote his bill down?

THESE ARE TRUE stories, stories that emanate not from one provider, but from many; not from one parent, but from many; and not from one well-intentioned legislator, but from many. Although their roles are distinct, these individuals are unified in their concern about the issue of early care and education (ECE) and its workforce. And they are not alone.

Because nearly two thirds of America's children under the age of 5 spend time in nonparental care, the national stake in the quality and effectiveness of ECE teachers is vast. Nearly 5 million individuals other than parents have the responsibility of caring for and educating young children (Burton et al., 2002). Although the adults who provide these services do so in a diverse array of settings (e.g., Head Start, public and private community-based child care centers, school-based prekindergarten programs, and home-based settings), their responsibilities are similar: to protect, nurture, and foster children's optimal growth and development. Their responsibilities are also complex: to consider educational theory and practice while addressing the needs of children, families, and communities each and every day. Finally, their responsibilities are significant: to work with children during the years when learning and development are most rapid and formative. Early childhood is the crucial period when positive interactions with adults can have the greatest impact on children's lifelong outcomes. For these reasons, the nature and quality of the ECE workforce are of paramount concern to parents, families, community leaders, and policymakers.

TERMINOLOGY MATTERS

One major challenge facing any effort to address the ECE workforce is the lack of definitional clarity about the terms used in research, analysis, and advocacy. As noted in the preface to this book, the field has been plagued with the inconsistent use of terms central to the topic at hand. To provide a crucial foundation and context, therefore, for the overall content of this volume, we begin with several key definitions.

> *Early care and education (ECE)* is a term that embraces different types of programs, all of which share the goal of nurturing young children's development, growth, and learning.

Center-based programs may be publicly and/or privately supported. They include Head Start, state-funded prekindergarten programs, nursery schools, and child care programs. They may be housed in schools, nursery schools, child care centers, or community/religious settings. A national study of center-based programs found that 29% of child care centers are for-profit programs, 22% are affiliated with a religious organization, 25% are independent nonprofit programs or are run by a public agency, 16% are public school-based, and 8% are Head Start programs (Saluja, Early, & Clifford, 2002).

Family child care (FCC) takes place in a home and usually is licensed by a state's child care regulatory entity, although states vary tremendously in the stringency and scope of their regulations.

Family, friend, and neighbor care (FFN) includes unregulated care provided either in the child's or the caregiver's home; this care often is legally exempt from state child care licensing regulations. Elsewhere, this type of service has been called informal care, kith and kin care, or license-exempt child care.

ECE teacher/s, or *the ECE teaching workforce*, as used herein, includes all personnel whose primary role is to provide direct instructional services for young children. Included in this category are lead teachers, assistant teachers, aides, FCC providers, and FFN caregivers.

ECE workforce describes those who carry out both instructional and noninstructional roles in ECE settings. Thus, the term *workforce* is an inclusive one that embraces teachers, others who work in ECE settings and whose primary responsibility is not instructional (e.g., administrators), and individuals who work in settings that support ECE (e.g., resource and referral coordinators).

TEACHERS MATTER

Contrary to many popular perceptions that the adults who care for and educate young children are babysitting, ECE teachers have tremendously complex and challenging responsibilities that occur at the most impressionable stages of children's development—the early years. There is no room for mistakes. Indeed, many studies, both experimental and quasi-experimental, have found teachers to be at the fulcrum of quality ECE and at the fulcrum of children's lifelong development (e.g., Schweinhart, Barnes, & Weikert, 1993). At the fulcrum, they balance many things simultaneously. First, ECE teachers must balance the demands of all the domains of young children's development, including physical and motor development, social and emotional development, cognitive development, language development, and approaches toward learning (National Education Goals Panel, 1994). They must weigh the needs of a group of children while supporting individual learners and balancing the interests of children, families, and communities (Feeney & Freemen, 1999). ECE teachers also need to balance children's different learning styles, using a variety of instructional strategies to connect with children who learn in different ways (e.g., cooperative learning, independent learning activities). In so doing, they balance different approaches to teaching (e.g., child-centered and teacher-directed) (Wien, 1995). They need as well to balance their roles as teachers in the classroom and advocates in the broader practice and policy world (Grieshaber, 2001). And of course, as Katz (2003) reminds us, ECE teachers must balance theoretical and practical knowledge in their interactions with young children.

Perhaps because teacher–child interactions are critical, even more so than classroom structure, in determining child outcomes (Love, Schochet, & Meckstroth, 1996), there is a good body of literature on the knowledge and skills possessed by quality ECE teachers. With regard to knowledge, consensus suggests that ECE teachers must have a comprehensive and current understanding of typical (Hutchinson, 1994; Kramer, 1994; Lobman, Ryan, & McLaughlin, 2005; Rowe, Early, & Loubier, 1994) and atypical (Isenberg, 2000) child development. They must understand how adults learn and how to work with families (Isenberg, 2000). ECE teachers also must understand the role of culture and cultural pluralism in children's development (AACTE Focus Council on Early Childhood Education, 2004; Isenberg, 2000; Kramer, 1994).

The skills that quality ECE teachers must possess are no less daunting. They must have the ability to observe and record children's learning (Bredekamp & Copple, 1997). They must be able to transform written curricula into effective practice for youngsters (Fein, 1994; Hutchinson, 1994; Isenberg, 2000; Lobman et al., 2005), use interactive routines to engage young children (Fein, 1994), and engage in thoughtful reflection that improves their ability to meet students' learning needs (Fein, 1994; Yonemura, 1994). And they must behave in ways that are highly professional (Feeney & Freemen, 1999; Isenberg, 2000; Kramer, 1994; Rowe et al., 1994). Indeed, much is demanded of quality ECE teachers.

CHALLENGES MATTER

Sadly, despite the knowledge about what constitutes quality teaching for young children, study after study demonstrates that there is a paucity of high-quality ECE teachers. Dubbed a national crisis in 1995 (Cost, Quality, and Child Outcomes Study Team, 1995), the ECE teaching workforce— not to mention the Emmas, the Lucindas, the Georges, and the Mikes —faces enormous challenges. Most challenges are deeply embedded in the fabric of America's approach to serving young children; as such, they need to be understood (and addressed) not as independent irregularities, but as systemic, structural, and ideological issues. Left largely unattended, these challenges have worsened over the years as ECE has expanded and high expectations for children and their teachers have been layered upon a largely unprepared workforce. Part II (Chapters 3, 4, and 5) of this volume details these challenges, providing both evidence and additional analysis of them. We preview them here to establish context for the remainder of this book.

Systemic Challenges

In order to understand the nature of the American ECE teaching workforce, one must understand the nature of American early care and education services—services characterized by inconsistency, fragmentation, and market failure. First, given the local nature of early childhood policy, there is no consistency across states or even within states regarding the way ECE programs are funded, regulated, monitored, or improved. At a basic level, such variation creates huge differences among states and among programs in ECE teachers' compensation packages and working conditions. Variation in states' and programs' teacher requirements and professional development opportunities further impacts recruitment and service quality. Moreover, access to professional development and opportunity for advancement vary among states and programs. Because these conditions vary, staff mobility is common, as is competition among programs for the highest quality personnel. Policy and program variation, then, wreaks havoc on teaching workforce consistency, quality, and stability.

Second, and equally problematic, there are few policy mechanisms that acknowledge and address the interrelationship among programs. When new funds are added to programs or when new programs are launched, rarely is there detailed analysis of the impact on existing programs and services. Little attention is paid to workforce demands and how expansion in one sector or type of program might affect other programs' teaching workforce issues (e.g., how the creation of prekindergarten programs may impact child care staffing, as in Emma's story). This lack of systemic planning further undermines quality and stability, leading some to assert that individual ECE professional development efforts must be coordinated with other ECE policies if they are to succeed. Couple the vast number of systemic irregularities with the lack of a consistent, sustained approach to policy investment and it is easy to understand why the ECE teaching workforce is so disjointed and uncoordinated (Kagan & Cohen, 1997).

Third, ECE operates at the intersection of the public and private sectors. As such, ECE is part of a market, albeit one that is highly imperfect (Mitchell & Morgan, 2000; Morgan, 2005). In a normally functioning market, a shortage of qualified personnel would increase compensation in the field. In ECE, however, employers respond to labor shortages by hiring from the virtually unlimited pool of under- or unqualified teachers. Because requirements to enter the field are so low, and because there is an unending supply of personnel, employers are easily able to keep compensation depressed. Classic market failure also is exacerbated when consumers do not have adequate knowledge of the product or service they are consuming, so they cannot easily discern quality. This diminishes market incentives to produce or enhance quality, and, with no incentives to improve, quality remains low. As consumers of ECE, many parents have difficulty distinguishing and affording quality. Under both conditions, their children often are placed in less than optimal care, further legitimating the demand for low-quality services. Comprehensive incentives to evoke better-educated personnel, higher wages, and, therefore, a more qualified teaching workforce do not exist in the ECE market.

Ideological Challenges

Looking beyond systemic issues, deeply held values and ideologies pervade the ECE field and conspire to impede significant advancement of the teaching workforce. In a country that values the privacy of the home and the primacy of the family, expanding early care and education services, and sending young children to formal out-of-home settings, are disapproved of by some. Although decreasing in number over the years, those who hold this opinion are unlikely to support public investment in young children, much less in the teachers of young children. Still others have deemed early care and education "babysitting," for which professional skills and professional wages are unnecessary.

Moving beyond these foundational ideological constraints, there are strong differences in ideas about what is needed to be an effective ECE teacher. The field continues to debate whether all teachers, across both the public and private sectors, can and should have the same entry requirements. In addition, there is little agreement on precisely what those requirements should be, with many advocating the necessity of a BA for all teachers, some advocating that each group of children have at least one teacher with a BA, and some advocating the AA degree (e.g., Barnett,

2003a; Whitebook, 2003). Related questions abound about whether quality teaching is best achieved via rigorous teacher entry requirements (suggesting more emphasis on preprofessional experiences) or via hands-on experiences teaching in an ECE classroom. If the latter, what should be the nature of these experiences (e.g., mentoring) and who should provide them (peers, professionals)? Ideological disagreements about ECE, then, range from the belief that it is inappropriate to the belief that it is essential. For those who deem it important or essential, ideology (increasingly buoyed by data) fuels debate on the precise nature of preparation that is necessary for the ECE workforce.

Structural Challenges

Emerging from systemic and ideological challenges, Emma, Lucinda, George, and Mike share the same plight; they all face endemic structural hurdles that frame their behaviors, choices, and results. In Emma's story alone, five structural challenges are manifest. She (1) never had stringent requirements placed on her as she entered the field, or even as she remained in it. She did her job for years without much recognition, (2) without any significant increased compensation that might bolster her wages and improve her personal and family well-being, and (3) without significant professional development. When an opportunity with higher pay, better benefits, and less responsibility came along, Emma wisely grabbed it. Thousands of Emmas unwittingly create (4) huge employee turnover, leaving their employers with a revolving door of personnel and (5) the associated challenges and costs of recruitment and replacement that turnover evokes. The structural challenges, then, are:

1. Low and inconsistent entry requirements and qualifications
2. Low compensation
3. Inadequate professional development opportunities
4. High turnover
5. Unsuccessful recruitment and replacement

But these aren't Emma's problems alone. Lucinda and George, even though they may not realize it, face serious challenges as well. The state-funded prekindergarten to which they are sending their eldest child requires certified teachers with BA degrees; the child care center where they are on the waiting list requires a credential called the Child Development Associate (CDA), which is roughly equivalent to the first year of college; and the family child care provider is not required to hold any degree or credential. The requirements and opportunities for professional advancement and increased compensation remain inequitable, favoring the adults in the state-funded prekindergarten program—the one to which Emma chose to move. But all is not well there either; teachers come and go in public schools (where many prekindergarten programs are delivered) and often those who are certified to teach older students are inappropriately placed in early childhood settings. Thus, the revolving door of personnel continues to rotate, with the consequence that Lucinda and George's children are not assured continuous care by providers who know them, their needs, and their families well. Indeed, the turnover of personnel may be jeopardizing the children's development, and Lucinda and George may not even be aware of these facts. Mike and policymakers like him from all over the country understand the challenges, in part because they are familiar with them in other industries, including K–12 education. The dilemma they face is knowing what to do about the challenges specific to ECE, actually doing it, and remaining in office long enough to complete the task.

SPECIFIC CHALLENGES: MAKING THE CASE FOR REVISITING THE ECE WORKFORCE

But just how pervasive are these challenges? Is this really a crisis? A brief overview of the challenges paints a compelling portrait of the gravity of the situation at hand. Each of these issues will be dealt with more fully in subsequent chapters.

LOW AND INCONSISTENT ENTRY REQUIREMENTS AND QUALIFICATIONS

- No matter what the sector, funding agent, or program sponsor, low entry requirements are common across the entire ECE workforce.
- In prekindergarten, 20 states require teachers to have a bachelor's degree, 16 states require teachers to have only a CDA, and three states require teachers to have an associate's degree in early childhood education (Gilliam & Marchesseault, 2005).
- In child care centers, only 12 states require teachers to have minimum education or training in early childhood development. Of these 12 states, two states require either a CDA or Child Care Provider (CCP) credential; four states require a credential plus experience; two additional states require the completion of a vocational child care program; and the remaining four states require some mix of education or training and experience (LeMoine & Azer, 2006a).

- Overall, 33% of center-based ECE teachers hold a bachelor's degree or more, 47% have some college, and 20% have high school degrees or less (Burton et al., 2002).
- Overall, only 17% of family child care providers have a bachelor's degree or more (Burton et al., 2002).

LOW COMPENSATION

- The median hourly earnings of child care teachers were $8.06 in May 2004 (Bureau of Labor Statistics, 2005).
- Just 22 occupations out of 820 surveyed by the Bureau of Labor Statistics reported lower mean wages than child care workers, with service station attendants, bicycle repairers, and locker room attendants earning more (Center for the Child Care Workforce, 2006a).
- In state-funded prekindergarten programs, which pay the highest wages in the ECE field, 13.9% of teachers reported a yearly salary below federal poverty guidelines, and 70.9% reported a salary below the threshold for "low income" (Gilliam & Marchesseault, 2005).
- Only 28% of the ECE workforce had employer-provided health insurance through their job, compared with 57% of workers in all industries (Herzenberg, Price, & Bradley, 2005).
- Few child care centers offer pension plans and fewer than 5% of center-based teachers have a union contract (Whitebook, Howes, & Phillips, 1998). The situation is far better among teachers in state-funded prekindergarten programs; in these programs, 88.7% of teachers were offered health insurance, and 79.5% were offered retirement benefits (Gilliam & Marchesseault, 2005).

INADEQUATE PROFESSIONAL DEVELOPMENT OPPORTUNITIES

- The supply of affordable and accessible educational opportunities to train personnel to advancing levels of competence is inadequate (Bowman, Donovan, & Burns, 2001).
- The systems of formal education and training—including the policies and programs that ensure the quality of ECE teacher educators and trainers, as well as the content of the formal education and training they provide—are inadequate.
- Even in states where adequate training opportunities exist, they are often inaccessible to ECE workers because of distance, schedule, and/or cost.
- The quality and content of training and formal education are highly variable, with little assurance that professional development actually translates into higher quality experiences for young children.

- Because professional development does not typically convert into increased salary and benefits, the incentive to undertake such additional work is understandably limited.

HIGH TURNOVER

- One third of ECE teachers leave their jobs every year; half of these leave the field altogether (Whitebook & Sakai, 2003).
- Higher staff turnover rates are associated with lower quality services (Cost, Quality, and Child Outcomes Study Team, 1995; Kontos, Howes, Galinsky, & Shinn, 1995; Whitebook, Howes, & Phillips, 1990).
- Specifically, high turnover is related to:

  fewer developmentally appropriate experiences for children;
  less responsive teacher–child interactions;
  poor structural indicators of quality (e.g., child to staff ratios); and
  more aggressive child behavior (Howes & Hamilton, 1993).

UNSUCCESSFUL RECRUITMENT AND REPLACEMENT

- ECE is losing many of its most qualified teachers to retirement or to the pursuit of other, more lucrative and prestigious options (Whitebook, Burton, Montgomery, Hikido, & Chambers, 1996).
- Often, those who replace seasoned caregivers are underqualified individuals who enter the field with limited education and/or relevant experience (Whitebook et al., 1998). Indeed, new teachers tend to be less qualified than those they replace (Whitebook, Sakai, Gerber, & Howes, 2001).

CONCLUSION

Today's ECE teaching workforce matters tremendously to the overall quality of the profession and to the outcomes achieved by young children. Indeed, as in every other industry, the teaching workforce is at the fulcrum of high-quality early care and education. There are, however, tremendous systemic, ideological, and structural challenges that destabilize the ECE workforce, undermining the hopes and intentions of teachers like Emma, parents like Lucinda and George, and policymakers like Mike. The importance of the ECE teaching workforce and the pervasiveness of the challenges it faces combine to substantiate an urgent need for comprehensive reform. If ECE teaching workforce issues are not addressed deliberately and comprehensively, the fulcrum will not be capable of balancing and sustaining the needs of children, families, and the economy. Without meaningful social change on behalf of the ECE teaching workforce, the promised gains of early care and education will go unrealized, as will the field's opportunity for change.

Tomorrow's Workforce Matters

JULIUS RICHMOND, to whom this book is dedicated, had an unrivaled career as both a renowned scholar and a public servant. Recipient of countless awards and author of scores of volumes, Richmond was one of the original founders of Head Start, Surgeon General of the United States, father of the American smoking cessation movement, and professor of health policy at Harvard. In these diverse roles, Richmond distinguished himself with his prescience and his cogent ability to take complex social issues and make them easily understood and actionable. Throughout his career, Richmond concerned himself with improving social conditions for all Americans. He had visions of comprehensive services to improve the lives of low-income and at-risk children; he had visions of creating a healthier America by establishing positive means to reduce smoking and its related illnesses. In pursuing his convictions, Richmond developed a comprehensive model of social change. As noted in the preface, this model proffers a codified knowledge base, substantial political and public will, and a clear social strategy as the three essential conditions for any social reform.

Like Richmond, we begin with a vision that establishes goals for the future of the ECE teaching workforce. Then, throughout the following chapters, we review the current status of Richmond's social change conditions, relating them to the ECE teaching workforce. As the volume unfolds, and based on our research and review, we present evidence that the first two conditions are nascent in the United States. We then offer a bold and comprehensive social strategy—a set of recommendations for ECE teaching workforce reform—that would render social change both possible and effective. To illuminate the line of argument we take in this book, we summarize in this chapter our vision and follow it with a preview of our recommendations, organized in accordance with Richmond's conditions for social reform.

VISION

If America wants a society in which young children are well prepared to face the challenges of formal schooling and life in a global society, we must transform ECE so it meets high-quality standards. Such ECE must be effective and culturally relevant; it must advance children's full development and ensure their positive outcomes. To do so, it must attract sufficient investment to have top-notch teachers who are as diverse as the children they serve, who are well trained, and who enjoy sufficient salary and benefits to ensure job stability without job stagnation.

In turn, ECE teachers must have confidence that their profession has a unified set of understandings about what children need to know and be able to do, and that their profession has an agreed-upon standard for certification and an established canon of ethics. They should be assured that the preparation they receive in institutions of higher education is current, relevant, and of high caliber. ECE teachers should have equal access to training that is linked to clear career paths, including opportunities for advancement and participation in management. They should be entitled to scholarship, financial, and career supports at least comparable to their counterparts in K–12 education and, given equal training and education, should be compensated at rates commensurate with those individuals. Finally, ECE teachers should work in supportive and inspiring workplaces that encourage communities of practice, reflective thinking, mentorship, and continued professional growth.

A CODIFIED KNOWLEDGE BASE

One purpose of undertaking the writing of this volume was to codify the existing knowledge base around the ECE teaching workforce. Elaborated herein, a great deal is known about who is teaching, what it takes to be a quality teacher, what supports must be provided, how to render appropriate professional development, and what new knowledge needs to be generated to refine, expand, and scale-up meaningful efforts to improve the ECE teaching workforce.

The field does not lack data on the ECE teaching workforce; rather, the data are abundant, confusing, and highly compartmentalized. First, most data on the workforce are not comprehensive; they exist only for particular types of programs or geographically limited (and often quite small) regions. Such lack of comprehensiveness prohibits ethical generalization about many critical workforce factors. Second, and equally problematic, is the lack of definitional and conceptual clarity around a number of key terms and concepts. Terms such as *teachers, workforce, professional development,* and even *early care and education* itself are used inconsistently by scholars. As a result, it is impossible to develop a cumulative knowledge base wherein data can be analyzed across settings, research studies, and time. Without a cumulative knowledge base, confusion will continue to reign, inhibiting integrated understanding, research, and policymaking. In order to create a codified knowledge base—the first condition necessary for reform of the ECE workforce—we make three recommendations.

First, we recommend that a working group of ECE experts convene to create a common lexicon and establish systemwide definitions to describe the field, its subsections (e.g., sector, program), roles within the ECE workforce (e.g., teachers, caregivers), and various forms of professional development (e.g., training and formal education).

Second, we recommend that considerably more attention be given to the understanding and development of an ECE system. Throughout this volume, we will note many outstanding practices, each of which contributes to its own locale. Often, however, these programs fail to produce outcomes of consequence because they function highly autonomously. They sit amidst an inchoate nonsystem of ECE that does not distinguish consistently the role of individual programs' functions within the broader ECE system; that does not differentiate roles of the federal, state, and local governments; and that has no consensus regarding the optimal relationship between the public and the private sectors. It is unlikely that workforce issues will be addressed equitably and comprehensively unless they are addressed systematically. To that end, we recommend that the National Academy of Sciences, as the nation's most prestigious scientific body, establish a panel to achieve greater conceptual clarity around systemic ECE issues.

Third, we recommend that the ECE research base be expanded dramatically through the comprehensive, recurrent, and sustained collection of data. As this volume will reveal, existing data are inconsistent; they do not pertain to the field at large, but to subsections of it; they are not focused on child outcomes; they rarely include cost–benefit analyses; they are not collected with regular periodicity; they vary by state in accordance with state mandates; and they do not address the entire ECE workforce. To fill these gaps, we recommend the establishment of a major publicly funded research entity. Called the National Institute of Early Care and Education (NIECE), this entity should: (1) collect ongoing surveys that report the status of ECE, (2) undertake research that evaluates the implementation and effectiveness of various reforms, (3) initiate and fund "ahead of the curve" research that furthers the practice of ECE, and (4) conduct or commission econometric research related to the advancement of ECE. Provisions within the NIECE should be made for the timely dissemination of usable research and for the training (through grants and fellowships) of the next generation of cutting-edge early childhood researchers.

By following these three recommendations, a durable and current ECE knowledge base would be developed and sustained. This knowledge base would inform the construction of sound and comprehensive social policy related to ECE and the workforce that serves it.

POLITICAL AND PUBLIC WILL

Unprecedented in American social history, today's calls for ECE are widespread. Hardly a governor, policymaker, police chief, or parent does not recognize the importance of the early years. In no small measure, this public and political understanding has come about, in part, as a result of the effective use of the media to garner public support for early care and education generally.

Unfortunately, as this volume will reveal, attention to young children is a mile wide, but only an inch deep. While the importance of the early years is acknowledged, there is little understanding of what it takes to produce high-quality early care and education, or the role that the workforce has in its production. Many promising strategies to improve the teaching workforce exist, but they have not been applied on a large enough scale to improve the ECE teaching workforce as a whole. To do this will require substantially increased public and political will.

To strengthen the second condition for social change—public and political will—there needs to be a means to take policies and programs that are effective, but only for limited populations, and expand them so they reach larger segments of the ECE teaching workforce. Increasing programs' reach and effect is a hallmark of public and political will, requiring investments of both human resources and funds. Many innovative state and local efforts that hold promise for large-scale reform are described in the following pages. We recommend establishing a major five-state demonstration effort whereby states interested in pioneering the linkage between the recommendations herein and their existing or planned efforts could contribute to a better understanding of how to build increased public and political will.

To further build public and political will, we recommend that a media campaign be launched and sustained in which a cadre of high-profile individuals (e.g., movie stars, corporate executives, policymakers), working in conjunction with the private sector, vocally and visibly emphasize and support the ECE teaching workforce as well as the programs that improve it. The campaign would pursue press and broadcast media strategies, with the goal of generating public understanding of the plight of ECE teachers and public support for comprehensive efforts to improve their professional development, certification, and compensation. Such an effort would use techniques that have proven successful in other social reform efforts. While having a well-timed launch, such a media campaign would be envisioned as an ongoing component of the overall reform effort.

A SOCIAL STRATEGY

Aligned with Richmond's third condition, the development of a clear social strategy, we offer specific, strategic, and, we hope, compelling action steps for the systemic improvement of the ECE workforce. Our analysis suggests three specific actions that would enhance the quality and the equity of the ECE teaching workforce.

First, we address the need to establish a more uniform ECE credential that would pertain to all ECE teachers in all settings. Throughout this volume, we repeatedly note both the importance of a quality workforce to positive child outcomes and the legion of problems caused by highly inconsistent, low, or even nonexistent entry requirements for ECE teachers. To both elevate and equalize entry requirements for ECE teachers across programs and across states, we recommend instituting a National Credential that all lead teachers in all ECE settings would need to possess in order to have primary responsibility for a group of young children. This National Credential would be awarded only after satisfactory performance on a new National Competency Assessment. Composed of a written test of knowledge and an observation of teachers' instructional competence, the National Competency Assessment would measure whether lead teachers have the requisite disposition, knowledge, skills, and abilities to work effectively with young children and their families. Similar to the nursing profession that administers its competency credential to individuals with an AA or BA degree, the prerequisite to take the ECE National Competency Assessment would be the completion of an AA or BA degree; upon successful completion of the National Competency Assessment, an individual with either formal degree could be credentialed as a lead teacher. These requirements would apply to lead teachers in centers and family child care homes, in for-profit and nonprofit settings, and in high- and low-ECE-spending states.

Second, both to support and implement the recommendation for a National Credential based on successfully passing a National Competency Assessment and to align the quality standards for institutions that provide training and education to potential and current ECE teachers, we recommend creating a National ECE Teacher Education Compact. The purpose of the Compact would be to: (1) set the standards for the National Competency Assessment, (2) administer the National Competency Assessment and credential teachers who pass it, and (3) ensure that the quality standards established for informal professional development, vocational-technical programs, and 2- and 4-year institutions of higher education are aligned with one another and with the National Competency Assessment. The Compact would work collaboratively with, and rely on the existing initiatives led by, the National Association for the Education of Young Children (NAEYC), the National Council for Accreditation of Teacher Education (NCATE), ACCESS (an association of ECE teacher educators in 2-year colleges), and the National Association of Child Care Resource and Referral Agencies (NACCRRA).

Third, adequate compensation for ECE teachers is necessary if we are to attract and retain quality teachers. To that end, we recommend the establishment of funding mechanisms that increase ECE teachers' compensation and comprehensive benefits. Fair wages, only one component of a compensation package, must be accompanied by financial assistance that encourages adults not only to achieve a level of training and education adequate to successfully pass the National Competency Assessment, but also to pursue ongoing training that keeps their skills and knowledge up-to-date. A comprehensive benefits package, including health insurance and retirement savings, is also necessary to raise the occupation of ECE teaching to a level commensurate with other professions. Three strategies warrant consideration. States could incorporate young children into their K–12 funding formula, thereby explicitly putting ECE on a par with K–12 and ECE teachers on a par with teachers of older children. Alternatively, they could increase and earmark individual and corporate income taxes, thereby distributing the tax burden equally between individuals and businesses, both of which would benefit directly from the expansion of higher quality ECE programs. Finally, states could expand and earmark payroll taxes, similarly distributing the burden between families and business but taxing only earned income.

CONCLUSION

As we look to the future, a quality ECE teaching workforce is essential to the advancement of early care and education. The recommendations we make are designed to build on Julius Richmond's understanding of how to bring about social change and are distributed among the need to build a knowledge base, to advance the political and public will, and to have a coherent social strategy. We do not claim that any particular recommendation is unique or new. Rather, based on the extensive study that follows, we are convinced that no broadly supported or coherent plan for improving the ECE teaching workforce exists. As both the research and the current practices demonstrate, there are good efforts, more in reality than in the research, but none of these can act to recalibrate a system that is resistant to change. By following a template with a proven track record, we believe that focusing simultaneously on the knowledge base, public will, and social strategy offers the best hope for enhancing the quality, compensation, and effectiveness of the ECE teaching workforce.

The Knowledge Base:
The Contemporary ECE Teaching Workforce

USING RICHMOND'S three conditions for social change, we begin with his first, the need for a codified knowledge base. To that end, all of Part II provides an overview of the existing knowledge base on the ECE teaching workforce. It does so in three chapters. Specifically, Chapter 3 provides a description of the individuals who constitute the ECE teaching workforce, reviewing teachers' personal attributes, professional qualifications, job stability, and professional affiliations.

Chapter 4 addresses variables related to ECE teacher quality. Because there is considerable confusion about, and failure to discern, the difference between teacher quality (i.e., what teachers do) and teacher effectiveness (i.e., the impact teachers have on improving child outcomes), much of the existing knowledge base examines clusters of variables that have been shown to evoke *either* quality *or* effectiveness. These variables include personal attributes, professional development and experience, job stability, compensation, professional affiliations, and work environment.

Turning from a focus on individuals, Chapter 5 explores the systemic impediments to building and sustaining a high-quality and effective ECE teaching workforce. The challenges facing ECE teachers include inequitable professional development opportunities, inadequate compensation, and poor working conditions. Furthermore, weaknesses in the ECE system—lack of cohesion, market conditions, and inadequate infrastructure—exacerbate these challenges.

We present this overview in order to illuminate the motivations for current ECE workforce improvement policies and practices and to inform the recommendations we make at the conclusion of this book.

A Portrait of the ECE Teaching Workforce

OF THE ESTIMATED 2.3 million individuals who are paid to teach young children, approximately 550,000 work in center-based programs, including public and private child care centers, Head Start, and prekindergarten programs; approximately 650,000 individuals work in family child care (FCC) programs; and another 1,102,000 individuals work as family, friend, and neighbor (FFN) caregivers. Within centers, about 50% of staff members are lead teachers and 40% are assistant teachers; the remaining 10% of staff are directors and therefore not part of the ECE teaching workforce as we have defined it (Burton et al., 2002). In FCC programs, 60% of teachers are designated as primary providers and the other 40% are considered assistants (Burton et al., 2002).

In looking at the characteristics of this ECE teaching workforce, many well-known and well-documented patterns emerge. ECE teachers are predominantly White women in their late 30s and early 40s (Saluja et al., 2002). Most ECE teachers have at least an associate's degree and earn salaries that are extremely low compared with those of individuals with similar qualifications in other fields. Because teachers are compensated so poorly, it is not surprising that turnover among the ECE workforce is high—almost twice the rate among K–12 teachers. A closer look, however, reveals that these patterns are not consistent across the various subpopulations of the ECE teaching workforce.

To begin to paint a portrait of the ECE teaching workforce, we discuss their: (1) personal characteristics, (2) professional development and experience, (3) stability, (4) compensation, (5) professional affiliations, and (6) work environment. Because sources for this knowledge base rely on different population samples and methodologies, inconsistencies in the data are prevalent. While we have tried to address these inconsistencies, it will become clear that greater codification of the knowledge base around the ECE workforce is needed.

PERSONAL CHARACTERISTICS

ECE teachers are alike primarily in one regard: gender. Estimates of the percentage of female teachers in the ECE workforce range from 95% to

99% (Child Care Services Association, 2004; Herzenberg et al., 2005; Saluja et al., 2002). This can be attributed to historical social factors: Women traditionally have provided care and instruction to young children. ECE teachers can be found in nearly every adult age group. Nationally, the average age of teachers falls in the late 30s and early 40s (Saluja et al., 2002). State-level data may differ from these national averages. In Missouri, for example, a study of teachers in child care centers and FCC homes found the age range from late 30s to early 40s to contain the smallest number of teachers; the largest number of teachers were younger than 34 (Gable & Halliburton, 2003). Teachers' age also differs according to program type. Home-based ECE teachers are generally older than center-based teachers: They are, on average, 44 years old, ranging in age from 18 to 79 years old (Layzer & Goodson, 2006). On the whole, as large numbers of those in the field approach retirement and fewer young people enter the field, the age of individuals in the ECE workforce is rising (Herzenberg et al., 2005).

Teachers' race and ethnicity differ according to state and program type, as well. A national sample of teachers in all types of center-based programs found 78% of teachers were White, 10% of teachers were Black, 6% were Hispanic or Latino, 1% were Asian or Pacific Islander, nearly 1% were American Indian or Native Alaskan; the remaining 4% identified themselves as mixed/other (Saluja et al., 2002). These averages, however, mask great differences among the states and among subsections of the ECE teaching workforce. For example, in 11 state prekindergarten programs in 2001–2002, 64% of teachers were White, 15% were Latino, and 13% were Black (Early et al., 2005). Head Start's teaching workforce was more balanced in its diversity; 36% of teachers were White, 28% Black, and 24% Hispanic or Latino (Hart & Schumacher, 2005).

Home-based caregivers are also a diverse population (Layzer & Goodson, 2006). In particularly diverse parts of the country like Alameda County, California, three quarters of FCC providers are women from minority racial or ethnic groups (Whitebook et al., 2004), with fully 20% Hispanic or Latina (Phillips, Crowell, Whitebook, & Bellm, 2003). A study of four midwestern states found that 58% of FFN caregivers were White, 36% were Black, 5% were American Indian/Other, and only 1% were Hispanic (Raikes et al., 2003). It is clear that there are major regional variations in race/ethnicity within the informal care segment of the ECE teaching workforce.

Although research has just begun to chronicle this, ECE teachers speak many languages. In a five-state study of state-funded prekindergarten programs, 32% of teachers reported speaking Spanish in the classroom and 5% reported speaking a language other than English or Spanish in the classroom (Early et al., 2005). Comparably, Hart and Schumacher (2005) found that 27% of Head Start teachers were proficient in a language other than English, although they did not specify whether teachers were native English speakers, whether they used languages other than English in the classroom, or which language(s) were currently in use. An in-depth study of center-based teachers and FCC providers in Alameda County found that, while 31% of the sample did not speak English as their native language, they all used English in the classroom (Phillips et al., 2003). More data are needed to get a clear picture of the FFN caregiver population.

The racial, ethnic, and linguistic diversity of ECE teachers, however, pales in comparison to the growing diversity of young children in America. Some research has explored the match between teachers' and children's ethnicity. The most comprehensive analysis of shared ethnicity comes from a national study of center-based programs done by Saluja and colleagues (2002). The study found that while 78% of teachers are White, the average ECE classroom comprises just 66% White children. However, the study found that in classrooms that contain a large number of non-White children, there is likely to be a teacher from the same racial/ethnic group that predominates among the children; similarly, classrooms in which 75% or more of the children are from one racial/ethnic group are likely to have a larger percentage of teachers of that same ethnic group than of another ethnic group (Saluja et al., 2002).

While in most cases teachers are more likely to be White than are the children they serve, there are several exceptions, notably, Head Start, FCC, and center-based classrooms in which 75% or more of the children are from one minority racial/ethnic group. In Head Start programs nationwide, the diversity of the staff generally reflects that of the children served, both in terms of racial/ethnic identity and in terms of the percentage of those for whom English is a second language (Hart & Schumacher, 2005). In a Massachusetts study of FCC homes and center-based programs, Marshall, Dennehy, Johnson-Staub, and Robeson (2005) found that only teachers in center-based settings are less likely to be Hispanic/Latino or Asian/Pacific Islander than are the children in their state. FCC providers in the state, however, have a racial/ethnic breakdown that mirrors the children they serve (Marshall et al., 2005).

PROFESSIONAL DEVELOPMENT AND EXPERIENCE

ECE teachers gain the knowledge, skills, and attitudes needed to instruct young children through multiple forms of professional development, including formal education, training, and credentialing (Maxwell, Feild, & Clifford, 2006). The data show that ECE teachers' professional development experiences vary tremendously.

General Formal Education

Formal education refers to the amount of credit-bearing coursework a teacher has completed at accredited education institutions, including 2- and 4-year colleges and universities. Formal education may or may not include studies related to child development and early childhood education; when it does, it is referred to as *formal education with ECE content*. Typically, data on formal education are reported in two distinct ways. First, data are reported based on the numbers of teachers who hold graduate, bachelor's, associate's, or high school degrees as their highest level of education. Second, data are reported according to job classifications.

In looking at the first, we see that teachers' formal education can be examined across program types or within program types. Among teachers in all types of center-based ECE programs, Saluja and colleagues (2002) found that 50% of teachers had a BA degree or more, 15% held an AA degree, and 20% held high school degrees or less. In a different national sample of center-based teachers and directors, however, only 30% of center-based educators had a college degree or more, 41% had an associate's degree, and 30% had a high school degree or less (Herzenberg et al., 2005). These results indicate that educational attainment varies according to the population sampled. Such variation is further evidenced when looking at teachers in all program types, but in diverse states. Reflecting major policy differences across the states, for example, 20% of lead teachers in child care centers and 39% of Head Start teachers in Massachusetts had an associate's degree (Marshall et al., 2005).

When considering particular program types, data on state-funded prekindergarten programs are prevalent. Within prekindergarten programs, one national study found that 73% of teachers held graduate or bachelor's degrees, 14% of teachers in state-funded prekindergarten programs had an associate's degree, and 13% held a high school degree or less (Gilliam & Marchesseault, 2005). By comparison, another study of six state prekindergarten programs reported that 59% of teachers held graduate or bachelor's degrees (Early et al., 2006). Turning from prekindergarten to Head Start teachers, 36% of teachers in Head Start programs in 2005 held a bachelor's degree or higher, while 33% had an associate's degree (Hamm, 2006).

The second way to analyze center-based teachers' formal education is to examine how educational attainment relates to job classifications. Looking at lead teachers in child care centers, for example, one study found that 33% held a BA or more; 47% had some college, including an associate's degree; and 20% had completed high school or less. Turning to assistant teachers, 12% held bachelor's degrees; 45% had completed some college, including an associate's degree; and 43% held high school degrees or less (Helburn, 1995). A more recent single-state study found roughly similar percentages (46%) of center-based assistant teachers holding high school degrees or less (Marshall et al., 2005). Surprisingly, when looking at state-funded prekindergarten programs, Gilliam and Marchesseault (2005) found a higher percentage (59%) of assistant teachers holding a high school degree or less as their highest level of education. This finding raises important staffing and class assignment questions, such as whether partnering lead and assistant teachers with (1) similar levels of formal education (two AAs, for example) or (2) discrepant levels of formal education (one holding a BA and the other a high school degree) is more likely to create high-quality early care and education experiences for young children.

In regard to home-based ECE settings, the data concur that education levels are even lower among FCC providers. One national study found that 11% of home-based providers held graduate or bachelor's degrees (Herzenberg et al., 2005). Data from a single-state study reflect national data, finding that 12% of FCC providers held a bachelor's degree or higher (Marshall et al., 2005). In four midwestern states, however, only 6% of FCC providers held a graduate or bachelor's degree and 41% completed some postsecondary education but did not hold a degree (Raikes et al., 2003). According to Brandon and Martinez-Beck (2006), the percentage of FCC providers with an associate's or bachelor's degree is not likely to exceed 10%–15% in any state. As expected, not only is the number of teachers with a college degree lower among FCC providers than among center-based teachers, but the number of providers with a high school degree or less is higher. A national study estimated that the percentage of the FCC workforce with a high school degree or less was 56% (Herzenberg et al., 2005). In some regions, though, the proportion of FCC providers with a high school degree or less is lower than the national average—32% across four midwestern states (Raikes et al., 2003) and just 28% in Alameda County (Whitebook et al., 2004).

Turning to the more informal home-based settings, studies of FFN caregivers in California found relatively high levels of education: 40% were found to have some college or a college degree (Drake, Unti, Greenspoon, & Fawcett, 2004). In Washington State, too, 40% of FFN caregivers were found to have some college attendance, including an associate's degree; however, the percentage with a 4-year college degree was low, at 14% (Brandon, Maher, Joesch, & Doyle, 2002). A similar pattern exists in four midwestern states, where 45% of FFN caregivers have some postsecondary education, including an associate's degree, but only 5% have a bachelor's or graduate degree (Raikes et al., 2003). Along with the relatively high levels of some college education among FFN caregivers, these states also have high percentages of FFN caregivers with a high school degree or less. In California, 40% of FFN caregivers did not graduate from high school (Drake et al., 2004); in Washington, 45% have a high school degree or less (Brandon et al., 2002).

In sum, what does this tell us about ECE teachers and their formal education? First, the amount of formal education varies by program type, with higher levels of formal education among teachers in programs that are publicly operated. Teachers in center-based programs have higher levels of education than their counterparts in home-based programs. Second, formal education levels vary by state, presumably because of great variation in state licensing requirements; only 12 states have any requirements for teachers' education in child care centers (LeMoine & Azer, 2006a). Finally, the amount of formal education varies according to the positions that ECE teachers hold, with lead teachers having higher levels of education than assistant teachers.

General Training

General training refers to all educational activities that take place outside of the formal education system. The structure of training varies but, according to Dickinson and Brady (2006), the "workshop approach" is the most common approach; support groups, seminars, videotapes, and participation in conferences are other common forms of training. Some training occurs in group settings, while other training occurs as one-on-one sessions or in a distance learning format (e.g., online courses, sequential videotapes). *Specialized training* refers to training in topics directly related to child development and early education. Training requirements and actual participation in training are crucial variables. Forty-seven states require teachers in child care centers to receive some form of ongoing training (LeMoine & Azer, 2006a). Twenty-three states with state-funded prekindergarten programs also have special regulations for annual teacher participation in training (Barnett, Hustedt, Hawkinson, & Robin, 2006). Across center-based settings nationwide, only 62% of teachers have participated in training (Saluja et al., 2002), suggesting that some ECE teachers may not be in compliance with regulations. Teachers in state-funded prekindergarten programs reported an average 32.9 clock-hours of ongoing training over a 12-month period, with hours ranging from 22.9 to 55.3 (Gilliam & Marchesseault, 2005); those authors note that this extreme variability can be attributed to the variation in state-mandated minimum levels of ongoing training for ECE teachers. A study by Epstein (1999) of teachers in three states found that Head Start teachers spent the highest number of hours per year in training (62 hours), followed by teachers in public prekindergarten programs (45 hours), with teachers in nonprofit child care centers having the fewest hours of training per year (27 hours).

It appears that FCC providers and FFN caregivers are accessing fewer hours of training opportunities than center-based providers. For example, a four-state study found that, on average, FCC providers participated in 19 hours of training and FFN caregivers participated in 16 hours of training annually (Raikes et al., 2003). A survey of FCC providers in Maryland showed that just one quarter had received training, although half said they were likely to participate in training in the future (Hamm, Gault, & Jones-DeWeever, 2005). Thirty-five states actually require FCC providers to participate in ongoing training (LeMoine & Azer, 2006b), but it is hard to say whether these requirements are being fulfilled. Among FFN caregivers, who typically have no training requirements, one state-level study in Washington showed that 61% had received no ongoing training (Brandon et al., 2002).

Credentials

Credentials document a person's completion of a set of requirements necessary to perform a specified function or role. *Credential* is a broad term that includes various types of certificates and licenses; a teaching license, nearly universally required in K–12 education, is perhaps the most commonly recognized credential in education. The most widely recognized, although not the only, credential in early care and education is the Child Development Associate (CDA); it is available to both center- and home-based teachers. The CDA is used by many ECE teachers as a means to improve their qualifications. Five states—Hawaii, Illinois, Minnesota, New Jersey, and Vermont—and Washington, DC, require teachers in child care centers to have at least a CDA or a Certified Child Care Professional credential (CCP, awarded by the National Child Care Association). One national study found that nearly one fifth of center-based teachers hold a CDA (Saluja et al., 2002). Among state-funded prekindergarten and Head Start teachers, the percentage is slightly higher: 23% and 22% have a CDA, respectively (Gilliam & Marchesseault, 2005; Hamm, 2006). While Hart and Schumacher (2005) found that 18% of Head Start teachers who do not have a degree or credential are enrolled in training for a CDA, Hamm (2006) notes that there has been a decline in the proportion of Head Start teachers with a CDA since 2002, when 35% earned the credential. This decrease may be attributable to the 1998 legislation mandating higher degrees for these teachers; that is, Head Start teachers may be pursuing associate's or bachelor's degrees rather than CDAs. Additionally, 3% of

FCC providers have earned a CDA, according to one multistate study (QUINCE in Workgroup on Defining and Measuring Early Childhood Professional Development, 2005).

Many ECE teachers hold state-issued teaching certificates, licenses, or endorsements (all forms of credentialing) that indicate they are qualified to teach young children. The scope of these credentials varies from state to state; for example, in 2006, Georgia's early childhood license certified teachers to work with children from prekindergarten through 5th grade, while the early childhood certificate in Illinois covered children from birth through age 8 (Barnett et al., 2006). One study of five states found that 57% of prekindergarten teachers were certified by their states to teach 4-year-old children (Early et al., 2005). Similarly, a national study of state-funded prekindergarten programs found that 57% of teachers hold a certificate to teach young children. That study found that regions with a higher rate of teachers with teaching certificates tended to be those with the highest proportion of prekindergarten classrooms located in public schools (Gilliam & Marchesseault, 2005). Among center-based child care providers, 44% have a state-issued teaching certificate; rates of endorsement and certification are significantly lower in FCC homes, with just 7% of FCC providers holding a state endorsement or certificate (QUINCE in Workgroup on Defining and Measuring Early Childhood Professional Development, 2005).

Experience

ECE teachers gain many of their skills on the job, accumulating experience the longer they stay in the field. Experience often is measured by the total number of years that a teacher has been teaching in the ECE field. Experience does not reflect the total number of years that a teacher has been teaching in the same classroom or program and, therefore, is not a proxy for workforce stability, which is discussed next in this chapter. Among teachers in state-funded prekindergarten programs nationwide, a little more than 8 years of experience teaching preschoolers is average (Early et al., 2005; Gilliam & Marchesseault, 2005). In California, a sample of center-based child care teachers averaged nearly 13 years of employment in ECE (Whitebook et al., 2001), while child care professionals (setting unspecified) in Florida have an average 11 years in the field (Evans, Bryant, Owens, & Koukos, 2004). In North Carolina, 58% of teachers in child care centers reported having been in the field for 5 years or more (Child Care Services Association, 2003). Nationally, FCC providers and FFN caregivers appear to have spent more years in ECE than teachers in center-based settings—19 and 22 years, respectively (Brown-Lyons, Robertson,

& Layzer, 2001). Brown-Lyons and colleagues suggest that this finding may be explained by the generally older population of FCC providers and FFN caregivers.

STABILITY

The stability of the ECE teaching workforce reflects the teacher turnover experienced by programs. Turnover is defined in two ways: *job turnover* refers to the rate at which teachers leave programs to take new positions within the ECE field, and *occupational turnover* refers to the rate at which teachers leave programs to retire or enter an altogether new field of work. Child turnover also exists; it refers to the rate at which children leave their programs or classrooms, and it is discussed later in this section.

While not providing direct measures of turnover, one set of studies has examined ECE teachers' length of tenure in their program. One national study, for example, showed that, on average, center-based teachers were in their current programs for 6.8 years; teachers in programs in public schools and religious settings were working in their programs the longest (7.8 years); and teachers in for-profit centers were in their programs for the shortest period of time (5.6 years) (Saluja et al., 2002). Among only state-funded prekindergarten programs, teachers averaged 5.8 years in their current programs and 3.5 years in the same classroom (Gilliam & Marchesseault, 2005). A related study, focused only on ECE teachers in California, found that center-based teachers were at their current programs for an average 5.7 years (Whitebook & Sakai, 2003). This study found that, among teachers leaving their jobs, approximately half left the field altogether (occupational turnover).

Perhaps the largest and best-known study providing direct measures of turnover in child care settings was conducted in California between 1994 and 2000 (Whitebook et al., 2001). Teachers and directors in 92 California child care centers were interviewed in 1994 and 1996; in 2000, teachers and directors in 75 of the original 92 centers were re-interviewed. Researchers found that 76% of teachers employed in the centers in 1996, and 82% of those employed in the centers in 1994, had left their jobs by 2000. Subsequent state and regional studies reveal even greater variation in ECE teacher stability. For example, in one Massachusetts study child care center directors reported that 26% of their teaching staff had left during the prior 12 months, while a second Massachusetts study found a turnover rate of 30% among full-time, center-based and Head Start teachers (Marshall et al., 2005). Data from North Carolina show that, on average, a comparable percentage of full-time teachers and assistant teachers

(24%) left their jobs over a 12-month period. However, the data indicate that centers experience divergent rates of turnover: 38% of child care centers had *no* full-time teacher turnover during the previous year, while 4% had turnover rates at or above 100% (Child Care Services Association, 2003). In Alameda County, turnover was found to be lower than that found in studies of other areas; in that county, less than one quarter of teachers in center and FCC settings left their jobs during a 2-year period. It should be noted, however, that Alameda County is relatively rich in resources for professional development, which could contribute to teachers' greater likelihood of staying in their jobs (Whitebook et al., 2004).

Turning to differences across program types and sectors, Bellm, Burton, Whitebook, Broatch, and Young (2002) compared turnover rates among public and private center-based programs in five states, finding that publicly operated prekindergarten programs have lower turnover rates than do privately operated programs. One likely reason for this disparity is that state-funded prekindergarten tends to pay higher wages than privately operated programs (Gilliam & Marchesseault, 2005).

Stability has different implications for home-based ECE teachers than it does for center-based teachers. In a center-based program, when a teacher leaves her position, a child will need to adjust to a new teacher but the ECE arrangement remains intact for the child and his or her family. By contrast, when a home-based teacher leaves her position, the child and his or her family must find, and adjust to, a completely new arrangement. Moreover, home-based teachers' reasons for joining and leaving the field differ from center-based teachers' reasons. Many home-based ECE teachers enter the occupation to care for their own young children and, consequently, may not approach their work with a high degree of intentionality (Kontos et al., 1995). When their own children become old enough for elementary school, some home-based providers may elect to leave ECE altogether, while others may pursue ECE as a long-term career (Nelson, 1990b).

Data on the stability of FCC providers are available from state-level studies. In North Carolina, FCC providers have a median of 5.4 years in business, and just 7% of FCC providers have been running their program for less than a year. By comparison, 26% of center-based teachers in North Carolina have been at their current program for less than a year (Child Care Services Association, 2003). Raikes and colleagues (2003) found that the majority (57%) of FCC providers in four midwestern states have been caring for children in their homes for more than 5 years, and the majority of these (59%) have been doing so for more than 10 years.

In a study of FFN caregivers in Washington State, 69% reported that they had been caring for the same child for 12 to 48 months, and 51%

had been caring for the same child for 24 to 48 months (Brandon, 2005). Stability data on home-based teachers, however, can be misleading. Turnover does not necessarily mean that the caregiver has stopped caring for children altogether; it could mean that she is caring for different children, which more aptly might be termed *child turnover*. Brandon (2005) suggests that caregivers are likely to stop caring for a child after 2 years—perhaps because parents have chosen to move the child to a different, more formal ECE setting, or because the child has become old enough to enter elementary school.

When looking at general ECE turnover, it is helpful to compare it with turnover in K–12 education. Such comparisons invariably yield the same conclusion; turnover rates among ECE teachers are exceedingly high. While in K–12 settings the total turnover rate is around 16% per year (Provasnik & Dorfman, 2005), in ECE settings the rate often is cited to be nearly twice that (Bellm et al., 2002). When distinguishing between job and occupational turnover, ECE mirrors K–12, where approximately half of yearly turnover is job turnover, while the other half is occupational turnover (Provasnik & Dorfman, 2005).

What accounts for turnover? The majority of studies indicate that wages are a significant factor—but not the only factor—that predicts turnover. Whitebook and colleagues (2001) found strong evidence for the link between wages and turnover: Centers paying higher wages had lower staff turnover, and centers with no staff turnover paid significantly higher wages than centers with turnover, even if that turnover was only at a moderate level. Teachers who earned higher than average wages were more likely to remain in their jobs. Notably, ECE teachers who left to take jobs in non-ECE-related fields earned significantly higher wages than those who remained in the ECE field. Working conditions and the overall quality of an ECE program also affect turnover rates. Lack of benefits, working in a climate with low stability of highly trained co-workers, experiencing a change in director, and working with a greater percentage of teachers who are not highly educated also contribute to high turnover (Whitebook & Sakai, 2003). Supporting the importance of center quality as a factor in turnover rates, a North Carolina analysis indicated that higher quality child care centers (as indicated by the state's quality rating system) had much lower turnover rates than lower quality centers (Child Care Services Association, 2003). Teachers who belong to a professional organization are also more likely to stay in their jobs (Whitebook & Sakai, 2003; Whitebook et al., 2001). Child care teachers themselves recognize the problem of turnover; 33% of those working in low-income communities said that the best teachers tend to leave "within a couple of years" (Light, 2003).

COMPENSATION

Compensation is a broad term that encompasses both the annual salary or hourly wages earned by ECE teachers and the benefits (e.g., health insurance, paid vacation and sick leave, retirement plans) that are accorded to ECE teachers. ECE teachers' compensation is notoriously low. A national survey conducted by the federal Bureau of Labor Statistics (BLS) distinguishes between "child care workers," defined as adults who primarily perform duties such as feeding, dressing, and overseeing the play of children, and "preschool teachers," defined as those who provide a more educational experience for the children in their care. A recent analysis of BLS data found the average yearly salary for preschool teachers in the United States to be $24,560, and for child care workers—including FCC providers—to be $18,060, just three-quarters of the salary of preschool teachers (Center for the Child Care Workforce, 2006a). Salaries also varied by geographic region: Average salaries for preschool teachers ranged from $17,880 in Tennessee to $36,120 in New York, while the average yearly salary for child care workers ranged from $13,770 in Arkansas to $22,200 in Massachusetts.

Although few national data exist, the benefits provided to ECE teachers are also meager. Only about 28% of center-based ECE teachers received health insurance from their employers in the years 2002–2004; during the same time period, 21% had no health insurance coverage at all (Herzenberg et al., 2005). State- and local-level studies reflect these national data. In North Carolina, for instance, just 14% of directors of center-based programs said their centers provided fully paid health insurance for teachers; 29% of teachers reported having no health insurance coverage from any source (Child Care Services Association, 2003). Whitebook and colleagues (2004) found that, in Alameda County, half of center-based programs offer fully paid health insurance.

While all ECE teachers suffer from inadequate compensation, disaggregating data according to program type reveals substantial inequity in teachers' earnings and benefits. Child care workers, those distinguished from preschool teachers by the BLS, earn more than only 22 occupations out of the 820 assessed; occupations with average earnings within 5% of child care workers include short-order cooks and parking lot attendants (Center for the Child Care Workforce, 2006a).

For teachers in state-funded prekindergarten programs, though, the picture is somewhat different. In 2003–2004, the average yearly salary for state-funded prekindergarten teachers was $30,998 (Gilliam & Marchesseault, 2005)—$6,438 and $12,938 more than the average salaries reported for "preschool teachers" and "child care workers," respectively, by the

Center for the Child Care Workforce (2006a). Even so, 13.9% of teachers in state-funded prekindergarten programs reported a yearly salary below federal poverty guidelines, and 70.9% earned a salary below the threshold for "low income" (Gilliam & Marchesseault, 2005). That said, because teachers in state-funded prekindergarten programs often are employees of K–12 school systems, they are much more likely to receive benefits. The same 2003–2004 national study found that 89% of teachers in state-funded prekindergarten programs were offered health insurance benefits and 80% were offered retirement benefits (Gilliam & Marchesseault, 2005). Another study, this one of five state-funded prekindergarten programs, found that 93% of teachers had health insurance and paid sick leave; 89% had a retirement plan; 69% had fully or partially paid dental insurance; 62% received tuition reimbursement; 58% had paid vacation; and 44% had paid maternity/paternity leave (Early et al., 2005). In a study of five different states, publicly operated state-funded prekindergarten programs were more likely to provide contributions to teachers' retirement and pension plans than privately operated programs. For health insurance, the percentage of publicly operated prekindergarten programs offering fully paid health care coverage ranged from a low of 29% in Georgia to a high of 91% in California, whereas the percentage of privately operated programs offering fully paid health insurance ranged from 0% in New York's for-profit universal prekindergarten programs (and 11% in its non-profit sites) to 60% in California (Bellm et al., 2002).

For the Head Start teaching workforce, the average annual teacher salary in 2005 was $24,608 (Hamm, 2006). Compared with state-funded prekindergarten teachers, fewer Head Start teachers receive benefits and, when they do, their benefit packages are less generous. In four midwestern states, 65% of Head Start teachers received health insurance and 48% received retirement benefits (Raikes et al., 2003). In Massachusetts, however, the situation was better: 97% of Head Start programs offered health insurance to full-time employees. For part-time employees in Massachusetts, however, the percentages were lower: 27% of centers and 63% of Head Start programs offered health insurance to part-time employees (Marshall et al., 2005).

Compensation information for FCC providers is available only at the state level, and only in some states. In terms of wages, in four midwestern states, FCC providers' average annual salary was less than half that of teachers in center-based programs—$12,740 in 2003 (Raikes et al., 2003). In Massachusetts, average wages of FCC providers are estimated to be $7.65 per hour (Marshall et al., 2005), whereas in North Carolina, the median hourly wage of FCC providers is estimated to be $5.71 (Child Care Services Association, 2003). In North Carolina, though, wages vary according to the quality of the provider's home; providers operating with a 4- or 5-star license (indicating services of higher quality) earned a median hourly wage of $6.53, while providers operating with less than 3 stars earned $5.32 per hour.

Turning to FCC providers' benefits, we note an important caveat. Because home-based providers are usually self-employed, they generally do not receive benefits from an organizational entity. FCC providers with benefits are likely to be paying the full cost of the benefits themselves or to be covered by a spouse's, partner's, or other family member's benefits plan. This is an important distinction from the employer-provided and employer-paid benefits discussed above. That said, in Massachusetts, 88% of FCC providers had health insurance from some source, often from their spouse's or partner's health plan (Marshall et al., 2005); in North Carolina, 70% of providers had such coverage (Child Care Services Association, 2003). In California, Whitebook and colleagues (2004) reported that 60% of Alameda County's FCC providers had health insurance coverage of some kind. More promising, a study of FCC providers from North Carolina, Texas, and California found that 80% had health insurance but just 54% had paid vacation, 55% had unpaid vacation, and 36% had some form of retirement benefits (Kontos et al., 1995).

Only about one third of FFN caregivers in the United States receive payment for their services (Brandon, 2005). Even then, their wages are the lowest in the ECE teaching workforce and put the caregivers below the federal poverty level. In four midwestern states, the annual salary for FFN caregivers in 2001 was only $7,920 (Raikes et al., 2003); the federal poverty level for even a single-person family in the same year was $8,590 (Department of Health and Human Services, 2001). In Washington State in 2003, the hourly wage for FFN caregivers ranged from about $2.60 to $5.00, depending on the age of the child (Human Services Policy Center, 2003); the minimum hourly wage was $5.15 per hour (Bureau of Labor Statistics, 2004). FFN caregivers' benefits are also low. Among nonregulated providers, 67% of nonrelative caregivers reported having health insurance from any source, 24% had paid vacation, 67% had unpaid vacation, and just 23% had a retirement plan. In the same study, 76% of relatives reported having health insurance, 4% had paid vacation, 63% had unpaid vacation, and 33% had a retirement plan (Kontos et al., 1995).

Across the ECE teaching workforce, higher wages are associated with higher levels of education. For center-based teachers in North Carolina, for example, the difference between having no college experience and having a BA or more was associated with a pay increase of 50%; for FCC providers in that state, the associated pay increase was 9% (Child Care Services Association, 2003). Research on Head Start shows that the average annual salary for a Head Start teacher with a CDA is $19,904; with a BA degree, that same teacher would earn, on average, $25,907, and with a graduate degree, over $30,000 (Hart & Schumacher, 2005). Despite being compensated for increased education, even Head Start teachers with the highest levels of education are paid significantly less than kindergarten teachers in public schools, who earned an average $45,250 in 2005 (Bureau of Labor Statistics, 2006a). Similarly, in North Carolina, the median wage of center-based ECE teachers is half the starting wage of public school teachers (Child Care Services Association, 2003).

PROFESSIONAL AFFILIATIONS

ECE teachers are often affiliated with two types of organizations: unions or professional organizations. National data suggest that less than 5% of ECE teachers are members of unions (Whitebook et al., 1990). Several national unions have ECE teachers as members, including the Services Employers International Union (SEIU), United Auto Workers (UAW), American Federation of Teachers (AFT), National Education Association (NEA), and American Federation of State, County, and Municipal Employees (AFSCME).

Not surprisingly, union participation varies by program type, with ECE teachers in state-funded prekindergarten programs having the highest levels of participation. National data suggest that in 2004, only 3% of the child care workforce were union members or were covered by a union contract, compared with about 14% of workers in all industries (Bureau of Labor Statistics, 2005). Higher percentages of preschool and kindergarten teachers were union members—about 17% (Bureau of Labor Statistics, 2006b). Increasingly, unions also are organizing FCC providers. SEIU counts over 90,000 FCC providers among its members. Union participation also varies by state. In Washington State, for example, 10,000 FCC providers are currently members of SEIU, and in Illinois 49,000 providers are members (Service Employees International Union, 2005). FCC providers in both states are permitted to participate in collective bargaining.

ECE teachers are also members of professional organizations. There are many such organizations, with two representing large groups of ECE teachers: the National Association for the Education of Young Children (NAEYC) and the National Association for Family Child Care (NAFCC). NAEYC represents nearly 100,000 members of the ECE workforce (National Association for the Education of Young Children, n.d.), while NAFCC represents more than 25,000 FCC providers nationwide (T. Chumas, personal communication, December 5, 2006); yet, association membership in NAFCC rarely exceeds 25% of regulated providers in a given locality (National Association for Family Child Care, 2006).

WORK ENVIRONMENT

Features of ECE teachers' work environment include the physical setting, the reward system, clarity about expectations and roles, decision making, supervisor support, and communication (Hatch, 2006; Stremmel, Benson, & Powell, 1993; Whitebook et al., 1990). Jorde-Bloom (1988) identified several additional features of the work environment that matter to teachers, including goal consensus, task orientation, innovation, professional growth, and collegiality. These features may interact to create a supportive work environment—or, if they are absent or in conflict, a discouraging one.

Compared with the research base on other characteristics of the ECE teaching workforce, few data exist on work environment. Those that do exist, show a need for improvement. To investigate ECE teachers' perceptions of their working conditions, Cornille, Mullis, Mullis, and Shriner (2006) surveyed 558 child care providers in one southeastern state. When asked to select their top three choices for work environment improvements, 36% of teachers chose increased supplies and equipment as crucial to their success as teachers; 27% requested more staff, 17% desired substitutes, 12% wanted to improve playgrounds, 12% preferred to stock a resource lending library, and 10% thought physical facilities or equipment could use improvement. While increased compensation was named most often among teachers' top three desired improvements (60% requested salary increases, and 38% wanted enhanced health insurance or benefits), it is clear that poor working conditions are a significant obstacle to teachers' classroom success.

In a similar study, Kontos and Stremmel (1988) evaluated teachers' job satisfaction in 10 ECE centers in urban and rural communities. They found that teachers generally were satisfied with their jobs, but one quarter were dissatisfied with the stress of working with children, and one fifth reported they were dissatisfied with administrative styles of their work setting. More important, general dissatisfaction with compensation, and little differentiation in teachers', assistant teachers', and aides' compensation and responsibilities, suggested that teachers have modest opportunity for meaningful career advancement; in other words, a career in ECE may be inherently dissatisfying given its structure. Other factors contributing to frustration and burnout include restricted decision making, lack of goal consensus, and long work hours; indeed, home- and center-based teachers alike take their work home with them, and younger care providers—those with children of their own—often struggle to maintain a work–family balance (Boyd & Schneider, 1997; Brown & Hallam, 2004; Nelson, 1990a).

While inadequate working conditions are experienced generally, one New York City study revealed that conditions varied according to program type (Granger & Marx, 1990). In programs sponsored by the Board of Education, teachers received one period of release time per week to devote to administrative responsibilities, two 40-minute periods each week to prepare for class, and priority in teaching assignment based on seniority among qualified applicants. The situation was worse for teachers in child care settings, who had 15 minutes per day of release time from instruction but did not receive paid preparation periods or choice in teaching assignments. Head Start teachers received no release time from instruction.

CONCLUSION

From all this information, we can draw some conclusions about the ECE teaching workforce. First, we know that it comprises mostly women who have generally low levels of formal education, and that programs tend to experience high teacher turnover. Second, we know that all of these characteristics vary across programs, and that the most notable differences are found between the most regulated type of ECE, state-funded prekindergarten, and the least regulated types, home-based FCC and FFN care. Beyond these generalizations, definitive conclusions are few.

It is difficult to get a clear picture of the national ECE teaching workforce because most studies do not look comprehensively at all program types, choosing instead to focus on just one or two (e.g., Head Start; private child care centers). State-level studies can fill some of the gaps in our knowledge. Throughout this chapter, we have discussed primarily work done in California, North Carolina, and Massachusetts, as well as the four states in the Midwest Consortium (Iowa, Kansas, Missouri, and Nebraska), which begins to give us some idea of what ECE teachers look like in different regions. Yet, the findings from state-level studies cannot be generalized to the national ECE teaching workforce; they come from states that are pioneers, devoting significant financial and conceptual support to the improvement of ECE and the ECE teaching in their states. Data from states that have invested substantially less in ECE workforce issues may look dramatically different.

One more major gap in the research describing ECE teachers is the glaring lack of data on FFN caregivers, followed closely by data on FCC providers. FFN and FCC represent the majority of ECE teachers (Burton et al., 2002), yet we know relatively little about them. Here, too, states like Washington and Minnesota are beginning to fill the gap. Yet, as noted above, findings from selected states do not substitute for a national perspective.

ECE Teacher Quality and Effectiveness

ALTHOUGH THE TWO are often confounded, in this volume, we distinguish teacher quality from teacher effectiveness. We define *teacher quality* as the positive actions and behaviors of teachers, and *teacher effectiveness* as the impact of teachers' actions and behaviors on the accomplishments of children they teach. We assume that teacher effectiveness is predicated on teacher quality, and acknowledge that a comprehensive knowledge base about the early care and education workforce must include an understanding of both. In part, this is due to the seminal role teacher quality plays in children's development; in part, it is due to the attention teacher effectiveness is receiving as part of the press for educational accountability. Indeed, the No Child Left Behind Act (NCLB) shines an intense spotlight on both measurable child outcomes and the "highly qualified" teachers who can produce those outcomes. Although the NCLB accountability requirements do not pertain directly to children in early care and education, the ECE community feels the press for accountability in recurring calls to (1) establish standards that help ensure children enter kindergarten with the academic skills necessary to succeed in school, (2) assess young children, and (3) raise ECE teachers' qualifications. But measuring teacher quality and teacher effectiveness is tricky.

Establishing valid measures of teacher quality is challenging because interpersonal relationships and interactions—highly subjective and context-dependent variables—are central to teaching. As a consequence, many studies use measures associated with program quality as a proxy for teacher quality. While measures of program quality sometimes include items explicitly related to teacher quality (e.g., warmth of interaction, attention paid to children, type of discipline used), more often they reflect structural factors unrelated to teacher–child interactions (e.g., classroom space, materials, schedule) or teachers' behaviors. Although program quality and teacher quality may correlate (Harms, Clifford, & Cryer, 1998), the use of proxy variables often leads to an imperfect and indirect assessment of teacher quality.

Measuring teacher effectiveness is even more challenging because it requires drawing conclusions about children's accomplishments and relating them to teachers' actions and behaviors. This, in turn, requires reliable observations of teacher practice, measurable and valid baseline and child outcome data, and evidence that the two are related. In addition to the already-noted challenges of measuring teacher practice, assessing young children is particularly problematic because of the variability of young children's responses, the limitations of available measures, and the way the measures are used and interpreted. Furthermore, there are many factors affecting children's accomplishments that are not dependent on teacher behavior (e.g., home and community environments, biological factors). As a result, assessing child outcomes and teacher effectiveness, particularly for any kind of accountability use, is most challenging.

Given these challenges, data on teacher effectiveness are limited. Although data on teacher quality are more readily available, neither data-base is robust. Despite these constraints, we report on a number of studies that relate the following variables to teacher quality (and, where feasible, to teacher effectiveness): (1) personal characteristics, (2) professional development and experience, (3) stability, (4) compensation, (5) professional affiliations, and (6) work environment.

PERSONAL CHARACTERISTICS

ECE teachers' personal well-being and beliefs affect their relationships with children and co-workers, thereby influencing their actions and behaviors in both classrooms and the overall work environment (Jorde Bloom, 1986). In particular, factors such as ECE teachers' motivation and commitment, their beliefs about young children's learning and development, and their psychological well-being contribute to the quality and effectiveness of their teaching.

Motivation and Commitment

Understanding why individuals choose to work with young children is important to understanding their actions and behaviors in the classroom. Teachers' commitment both to children and to the community matters. Commitment to caring for children fosters stability and consistent, warm relationships between children and their teachers (Weaver, 2002b). In looking specifically at child care teachers' motivations for continuing to teach, however, Howes, James, and Ritchie (2003) found that those who stayed "for the community" felt a responsibility for creating and maintaining a network that would support themselves and others in the community. These teachers were more likely to be responsively involved with children, engage in language play, and provide language arts activities than those who stayed "for the children." Teachers who are committed to teaching "for the community," then, promote both a short-term dedication to caring for children and a long-term investment in child and community well-being.

As part of a larger report on the human services workforce, one survey polled child care teachers, asking them about their motivations to come to work each day (Light, 2003). Forty-six percent of the child care teachers who serve low-income communities responded that they came to work each day because of the nature of the job; 56% of teachers serving higher income communities gave the same response. Eighteen percent of those working in low-income communities said they came to work for the common good, compared with 10% of those working in higher income communities. Finally, a small percentage of each group answered that they came to work because of the compensation—8% in low-income communities and 10% in higher income communities.

Beliefs

There is general agreement that teachers' beliefs about young children's learning and development correspond with the quality of their interactions with children. Nonauthoritarian child-rearing beliefs consistently are associated with positive teacher behaviors in center- and home-based ECE (National Institute for Child Health and Human Development Early Child Care Research Network, 1996) and with teachers' daily practice (Bowman et al., 2001).

Often teacher beliefs are deeply entrenched and difficult to change because they were developed during teachers' own childhoods, reflecting the interactions they had with their own teachers and other adults (Lortie, 1975). Such beliefs influence how malleable teachers are in their daily practice, with beliefs often influencing teachers' ability to incorporate new educational practices (Ball & Cohen, 1996; Kennedy, 1997). Although both preservice and inservice professional development programs address teachers' beliefs about teaching and learning, research has long suggested that many teachers do not incorporate the practices and research learned in these programs into their own instruction unless the new knowledge fits with their already-formed beliefs (Bowman et al., 2001). Because views about teaching and learning can be so difficult to change, it is important that teachers "develop the ability to reflect on their beliefs, and . . . cultivate the metacognitive capacities that will help tailor their teaching strategies and approaches to the needs of their students" (Bowman et al., 2001, p. 267).

Psychological Well-Being

Teachers' psychological well-being impacts their work, particularly because of the highly interactive nature of quality teaching. Research indicates that teachers with higher levels of depressive symptoms tend to have lower quality interactions with children (Hamre & Pianta, 2004). For example, teachers who reported higher levels of depressive symptoms were rated by observers as being less sensitive and more withdrawn than teachers reporting lower levels of depressive symptoms; they also tended to spend less time engaged with children. While this is the only study we found that specifically examines the relationship between teachers' depressive symptoms and teachers' interactions with children, other research looks at the relationship between teachers' emotional well-being and turnover. In Whitebook and colleagues' (2004) study of center- and home-based child care teachers in Alameda County, California, higher levels of depression were positively associated with teachers' decisions to leave the field.

Unfortunately, depressive symptoms may be relatively common among ECE teachers. In a study of child care professionals in Florida, 80% reported experiencing low levels of personal accomplishment and 45% reported moderate or high levels of emotional exhaustion; another 14% reported moderate or high levels of depersonalization (Evans et al., 2004). Eleven percent reported moderate or high levels of all three symptoms. Many ECE teachers face taxing emotional challenges that reflect a complex combination of factors. Some researchers, for example, link low psychological well-being to the fact that many ECE teachers and caregivers are low-income mothers, a population that generally reports elevated levels of depressive symptoms, and, as a result, emotionally negative parenting styles; negative teaching styles may accrue from depressive symptoms, as well (Raver, 2003).

PROFESSIONAL DEVELOPMENT AND EXPERIENCE

Research has shown that teachers' knowledge and skills correlate strongly with the quality and effectiveness of their teaching. Here, we examine research that addresses how the various types of professional development—formal education, training, and credentialing—and professional experience impact teacher quality and effectiveness. First, we address general formal education and training, those educational experiences that are not specifically related to child development or early care and education. We then turn to specialized formal education and training, those experiences that specifically emphasize child development and/or early care and education.

General Formal Education

Formal education refers to coursework for which credits are received provided in an accredited educational institution, including 2- and 4-year colleges and universities. Many studies have correlated teachers' level of formal education with the quality of their teaching (Barnett, 2003a; Tout, Zaslow, & Berry, 2006; Whitebook, 2003). Some research links higher formal education levels among teachers to higher quality programs and more positive teacher–child interactions (Howes, 1997; Tout et al., 2006). In particular, these studies assert that college education—specifically, a 4-year college degree—contributes to optimal teacher behavior (Barnett, 2003a; Whitebook, 2003). A recent study by researchers at the National Center for Early Development and Learning, however, complicates the claim. This study examined the relationship between teachers' formal education and children's academic outcomes in more than 200 state-funded prekindergarten classrooms in six states. Findings suggest that there is little to no correlation between teachers' years of education and children's achievement, and only a marginal association between years of formal education and teacher quality, as measured by the Early Childhood Environment Rating Scale (ECERS-R) (Early et al., 2006). To date, then, research neither confirms nor denies that a BA is essential for teacher quality or effectiveness.

As a result, just how much, or what kind of, formal education matters remains an unanswered question. Research has not yet systematically examined formal education thresholds, the relative value of attaining specific minimum levels of education, certification, or training for teacher quality or child outcomes (Tout et al., 2006). The role of selection bias in the acquisition of formal education also is unknown; the qualities that motivate a teacher to pursue additional education and that allow a teacher to pursue formal education may be the very same qualities that make a teacher more effective in the classroom (Tout et al., 2006). For example, an ECE teacher may feel that teaching young children is not merely a job, but a calling. This inspiration may motivate her not only to provide children with the highest quality experiences, but also to pursue a bachelor's degree. The same bias may apply to those teachers seeking training and credentialing opportunities.

Despite these gaps in the knowledge base, some research does point to positive effects of formal education on specific variables related to child outcomes. For example, Howes and colleagues (2003) looked at the relationship between teachers' formal education and language and literacy activities in the classroom. They found that teachers with a bachelor's degree provided more language activities and language play than teachers with less formal education; however, it should be noted that the study examined only the quantity of language activities, not their content or quality. An earlier study by Howes (1997) showed that more formal education among teachers is positively related to children's language acquisition —a finding that relates directly to specific child outcomes and, therefore, to teacher effectiveness.

Other studies have examined the effects of formal education on teacher–child interactions, including such variables as sensitivity, interaction style, and responsiveness. One study found that centers with a higher percentage of teachers with bachelor's degrees received better ratings on measures of teacher sensitivity than did centers with fewer bachelor's level teachers (Whitebook et al., 2004). In another study, teachers demonstrating a positive interaction style were more likely to have a college degree than were teachers who had a more controlling interaction style (de Kruif, McWilliam, Ridley, & Wakely, 2000). Finally, research shows that teachers with bachelor's degrees exhibit more-responsive involvement with children than teachers with lower levels of formal education (Howes et al., 2003).

Other research has examined the relationship between teachers' level of formal education and their philosophy of teaching. McMullen and Alat (2002) looked at a small sample of ECE teachers in Indiana and found that teachers with bachelor's degrees are more likely to adopt a philosophy of teaching that incorporates developmentally appropriate practice (DAP) than are teachers with less formal education, confirming earlier findings from the National Child Care Staffing Study (Whitebook, Phillips, & Howes, 1993). ECE programs founded on the principles of DAP generally are believed to provide a high-quality educational experience for young children (National Association for the Education of Young Children, 1996); however, whether teachers who subscribe to DAP philosophy are better teachers is debated (e.g., Bowman et al., 2001).

The impact of teachers' formal education differs between center-based and home-based programs. In center-based programs, better-educated staff may be able to compensate for the shortcomings of less-educated staff. In contrast, in FCC homes, the educational background of an individual provider may play a more significant role in determining quality, primarily because there often is only one provider in an FCC home (Whitebook et al., 2004). Indeed, research shows that better-educated FCC providers maintain higher quality environments (Burchinal, Howes, & Kontos, 2002; Clarke-Stewart, Vandell, Burchinal, O'Brien, & McCartney, 2002; Weaver,

2002b). A study of FCC providers in 10 states found that providers with higher levels of formal education scored higher on the Child Care Home Observation for Measurement of the Environment (CC-HOME), a measure that looks broadly at the quality of the home environment (Clarke-Stewart et al., 2002). Specifically, providers who had attended college performed better than providers who had a high school degree but no college experience, and providers with a high school degree but no college experience performed better than providers without a high school degree. FCC providers with more formal education also scored higher on measures of positive caregiving, as defined by the Observational Record of the Caregiving Environment (Clarke-Stewart et al., 2002). In addition, providers with more formal education have been found to score lower on measures of punitiveness and detachment, and to be better facilitators of children's social and intellectual growth than providers who have less formal education (Weaver, 2002b).

Looking specifically at the relationship between FCC providers' formal education and child outcomes, Clarke-Stewart and colleagues (2002) analyzed data from the National Institute of Child Health and Human Development (NICHD) Study of Early Child Care and found that children in the care of providers with college experience scored higher on cognitive tests than children whose providers had not attended college. Among FCC providers, then, there is some evidence of a relationship between formal education and teacher effectiveness.

General Training

Apart from formal education, training also can impact teacher quality. Training includes educational activities that take place outside of the formal education system. Most research on this topic examines how much training teachers have received, often without examining the independent effects of the nature, process, or specific content of the training. As a result, we do not know, for example, whether workshops (the type specified most often) are more beneficial to teachers than other types of training, such as professional conferences or sequential vocational courses. The importance of *how* training is delivered, in addition to *how much* is delivered, may explain some of the equivocal results described below.

Honig and Hirallal (1998) conducted a study in which they classified center-based teachers as "high" or "low" in three categories: formal education, training, and experience. They found that training, independent of education and experience, had a large impact on the quality of services provided by teachers. Teachers in the "high training" group, those who had attended five or more workshops or training courses, were more likely to have positive language interactions with children, facilitate children's language development, give greater support for concept learning, and demonstrate supportive behavior that promoted children's social and physical skills, when compared with teachers who had attended fewer than five workshops or training courses. Despite the small sample size ($N = 81$), this study demonstrates the importance of training for center-based ECE teachers.

In a Florida study, teachers in child care centers who reported having more training were shown to plan more activities for children in their classrooms than teachers with less training (Ghazvini & Mullis, 2002). A small set of studies has looked at training while controlling for level of formal education, finding that training does make a unique difference in the level of quality of center-based settings (Tout et al., 2006). For example, a four-state study found that teachers' attendance in workshops was a predictor of both global quality and children's outcomes, specifically children's receptive language abilities (Burchinal, Cryer, Clifford, & Howes, 2002). This study points to a compelling, albeit limited, relationship between teachers' training and teacher effectiveness.

Research has been done on training as it relates specifically to the quality of FCC homes. In these settings, as in center-based settings, training has been found to correlate with higher scores on measures of global quality (Burchinal, Cryer, et al., 2002; Clarke-Stewart et al., 2002; Norris, 2001). FCC providers who participated regularly in training over the course of their careers maintained a greater variety of materials and activities, balanced children's time spent indoors and out, and were more likely to interact actively with children (Norris, 2001). Providers who attended more training workshops also have received higher scores on positive caregiving measures (Burchinal, Cryer, et al., 2002). While Kontos, Howes, and Galinsky (1996) found that specific training improved FCC providers' program quality (e.g., safety and healthfulness of environment, type of stimulation provided), it did not change the quality of the providers' interactions with children (e.g., sensitivity, harshness, detachment, responsive involvement). Regarding teacher effectiveness and child outcomes, one study found that FCC providers who had higher levels of education and also participated in training in the past year cared for children who scored higher on cognitive tests (Clarke-Stewart et al., 2002).

Specialized Formal Education and Specialized Training

While the evidence above indicates the importance of teachers' having general formal education and/or training, research has not examined systematically the relative impact of general education and training versus specialized education and training. As already noted, in this volume we define *specialized formal education and training* as professional development that includes specific emphasis on child development and early care and education. It is not known, for example, whether a BA in anthropology leads to the same outcomes for children as does a BA in child development. Because most ECE teachers with advanced degrees receive their degrees in an ECE-related field, it is nearly impossible to parse out the differential effects of the degree and the ECE content knowledge (Early et al., 2006). Moreover, it is unclear whether a BA in child development from one institution of higher education is equivalent in both content and quality to the same degree from another institution.

Researchers who examine the impact of teachers' knowledge of child development on classroom practices do so by looking at teachers' training and education that is explicitly focused on child development (Tout et al., 2006). Overall program quality is greater when teachers receive more specialized training and/or education with child development content (Blau, 2000; Phillips, Mekos, Scarr, McCartney, & Abbott-Shim, 2001; Tout & Zaslow, 2004). Child development-specific coursework or training improves teacher quality, as well (Berk, 1985; McMullen & Alat, 2002; Ruopp, Travers, Glantz, & Coelen, 1979; Whitebook et al., 2004). Specialized formal education, in particular, also appears to have a positive effect on teacher quality. For example, Howes (1997) found that teachers who had more child development education were more sensitive, less harsh, and more responsive to children. Similarly, center-based child care teachers with specialized education and training demonstrated more positive management in the classroom and participated in more language play with children than did teachers without such education and training (Howes, 1997). One of the difficulties in discerning the importance of these studies is the lack of clarity about whether it was the specialized formal education, the specialized training, or the combination that made a positive difference in teacher quality.

Data about the importance of specialized formal education and training are scarce for home-based providers. One study shows that FCC providers who have college coursework or a degree in ECE maintained higher quality settings than those without college coursework in ECE (Weaver, 2002a).

Credentials

Credentials document a person's completion of a set of requirements necessary to perform a specified function or role; the term includes various types of certificates and licenses. As noted in Chapter 3, the most widely recognized credential in early care and education is the Child Development Associate (CDA). Given the prevalence of the CDA, surprisingly little research has evaluated its relationship to teacher quality and effectiveness (Tout et al., 2006). In one study, center-based child care teachers who had a CDA were more sensitive than teachers with some college-level ECE coursework and teachers who had graduated from high school and participated in ECE workshops. These same teachers with CDAs also engaged in more language play and positive management than teachers with a high school education. In the same sample, however, teachers with a bachelor's degree were more sensitive than those with a CDA (Howes, 1997). One study of prekindergarten teachers is beginning to suggest a relationship between the CDA and center-based teachers' effectiveness; even though children who have prekindergarten teachers with high school or AA degrees *and* a CDA do not show gains on standardized assessment measures, they do show gains in rhyming and identification of letters, numbers, and colors (Early et al., 2006). As elsewhere in this chapter, these results show limited, but evident, correlations between the CDA and teacher effectiveness.

A study of FCC providers in Wisconsin (Weaver, 2002a) looked at the relationship between the CDA plus accreditation (as a combined variable) and FCC quality. While the research did not highlight the isolated effect of the CDA on teacher quality or effectiveness, it did find a significant association between a provider's possession of the CDA and/or accreditation and the global quality of the provider's FCC home, as measured by the Family Day Care Rating Scale (FDCRS; Harms & Clifford, 1989). Specifically, the study found that the CDA and/or accreditation led to greater global quality than did meeting yearly training requirements without achieving this particular credential or accreditation.

Experience

While most research has shown that teachers' years of experience in the ECE field do *not* predict the quality of their teaching practices (Honig & Hirallal, 1998; Kontos et al., 1995; Whitebook et al., 1990), the knowledge base is not uniform. For example, McMullen (2003) found that more experienced teachers believed more strongly in developmentally appropriate practice (DAP) and more frequently engaged in DAP than teachers with less experience in the field. While this study seems to link experience with teacher quality, confounding variables, particularly compensation (because teachers with more experience are likely to be paid more), complicate the findings. A study of state-funded prekindergarten programs that addressed both experience and compensation, however, suggests that experience matters. It found that classrooms with a positive emotional climate and high instructional quality were led by teachers with more experience, lower wages, and lower levels of formal education than teachers in those classrooms that had a positive emotional climate and only mediocre instructional quality (LoCasale-Crouch et al., 2007). As with training and formal education, the *how* of experience—the kind of professional development teachers engaged in during their years of ECE, or why they remained in their positions, for example—more than the *how long*, may explain these equivocal results.

Mentorship

In this book, mentorship describes the professional support and encouragement shared with an ECE teacher, over a period of time, by a qualified supervisor. There has not been a major national study of mentorship in ECE; thus, the knowledge base is limited to samples from small communities or single states. Although the research base is modest, mentorship appears to be positively related to teacher quality and effectiveness. One study found that teachers who were mentored early in their careers demonstrated greater responsive involvement in the classroom than teachers who had not received such mentorship (Howes et al., 2003). Another study divided a small random sample of infant-toddler teachers into two groups: one that received 4 months of mentorship and one that did not. In this study, the mentor observed the teacher extensively and then collaborated with her to address challenges. Positive changes did occur in the classrooms of the teachers who received mentorship: Subscales of the Infant/Toddler Environment Rating Scale (ITERS; Harms, Cryer, & Clifford, 1990) showed statistically significant improvement in areas such as learning activities, sensitivity, appropriate discipline, and routines (e.g., mealtimes, naptime, diapering/toileting) (Fiene, 2002).

Another study examined the effects of teacher mentorship on child outcomes and found that children in classrooms with teachers who received mentoring made greater gains on several measures of the Family and Child Experiences Survey (FACES) and on the Child Assessment Battery than did children whose teachers did not receive mentoring (Lambert et al., 2006). The mentoring program also affected teacher quality as measured by the Assessment Profile for Early Childhood Programs, which is designed to measure the quality of classroom teaching practices and procedures. Interestingly, teachers who did not participate in the mentoring program showed significant declines on most of the assessment's scales (Lambert et al., 2006). Much like other research presented in this chapter, these findings may reveal positive effects of mentorship on both teacher quality and teacher effectiveness, but they are limited in both scale (only one study in the research base) and scope (the outcomes measured were specific items on specific scales).

STABILITY

As noted previously, teacher stability refers to both job turnover, the rate at which teachers leave their program, and occupational turnover, the rate at which they leave the field altogether. Stability impacts overall program quality (Cost, Quality, and Child Outcomes Study Team, 1995; Phillips et al., 2001; Whitebook & Sakai, 2003), creating enormous costs for ECE programs, including those associated with recruiting and training new teachers. When the turnover rate is high in a particular program, it disrupts the organizational culture and creates an extra burden for those teachers who remain, thereby resulting in reduced quality of services (Seavey, 2004) and an increased likelihood that other teachers also will leave the program (Whitebook & Sakai, 2003).

Stability also impacts teacher quality (Cost, Quality, and Child Outcomes Study Team, 1995; Phillips et al., 2001; Whitebook & Sakai, 2003), with some negative costs being borne by young children. In one study, for example, children in centers with high staff turnover spent less time in social activities with peers and more time in "aimless wandering" (Whitebook et al., 1990). Turnover is likely to have the most direct effect on child outcomes when children experience unpredictable teacher changes. This type of turnover prevents the development and maintenance of consistent relationships that are so important to children's sense of security (Whitebook & Sakai, 2003). In making links between teacher stability and child outcomes, one study showed that children in centers with high turnover scored lower on language assessments than children in centers with greater teacher stability (Whitebook et al., 1990). Another study showed that children with unstable ECE arrangements tend to have more behavioral problems and poorer school adjustment in first grade as compared with children with more stable arrangements (Weber, 2005).

Turnover is a more complicated construct than it initially appears. Research on the effects of turnover has led many to view turnover as inherently negative, yet this is not always the case (Whitebook & Sakai, 2003). As alluded to above, there may be a difference in the effects of predictable year-end teacher turnover and unpredictable mid-year turnover (Weber, 2005). Moreover, when a teacher moves up the career ladder to become the director of a child care center, this may be a positive step for that teacher and for the workforce. Stability, then, should not be promoted to the point of professional stagnation; as Whitebook and Sakai (2003) aptly put it, the ECE workforce would benefit from a balance between negative turnover (when teachers leave their jobs even though they would prefer to stay) and negative stability (when teachers stay in their jobs even though they would prefer to leave).

COMPENSATION

Compensation comprises the annual salary or hourly wages earned by ECE teachers and the benefits (e.g., health insurance, paid vacation and sick leave, retirement plans) accorded to teachers. Both salary/wages and benefits influence teacher quality. Looking at wages first, teachers who are poorly paid tend to work in lower quality programs that provide a poorer educational experience for children; conversely, teachers earning higher wages have been linked to higher program quality, even when structural features such as student–teacher ratios are controlled (Barnett, 2003b; Cost, Quality, and Child Outcomes Study Team, 1995; Whitebook et al., 1990). In fact, one study found that teacher wages were the strongest predictor of classroom quality in child care centers, stronger than any other structural indicator at either the center or classroom level (Phillips et al., 2001). The link between teachers' wages and classroom quality may be mediated by job stability: Teachers who earn higher wages are more likely to stay in their jobs (Whitebook et al., 1998; Whitebook et al., 2001), and, as already noted, this stability of the teaching workforce is related to both teacher quality and child outcomes.

Despite this evidence, the research is not unanimous on the correlation between wages and teacher quality. One study, for example, refutes the claim that salary plays such an integral role in the quality of the classroom experience. Blau (2000) reanalyzed the four-state data from the Cost, Quality and Child Outcomes study, using different statistical techniques, and found that teachers' wage rates had no relationship with quality. Similar conclusions have been drawn from research in elementary and secondary education, where increased teacher salaries do not appear to improve student outcomes (Hanushek, 1997). Given the exceedingly low wages earned by many ECE teachers in the first place, though, these findings should not be construed to mean that wages do not matter at all.

Turning now to benefits, better and more comprehensive benefits increase teachers' nonwage compensation and, logically, contribute to greater job stability and lower turnover (Whitebook et al., 2001). Research indeed has found that benefits, particularly health insurance and pension plans, influence teachers' decisions to stay at or leave their centers. When asked for their suggestions about reducing turnover, 75% of center-based

ECE teachers who left their jobs between 1994 and 2000 recommended improving benefits (Whitebook & Sakai, 2003). The effects of benefits on quality, therefore, may operate indirectly through their effects on overall compensation and stability. As described previously, lowering turnover consistently predicts better child outcomes. Unfortunately, empirical research has not examined the direct association between employment benefits and teacher quality or teacher effectiveness.

PROFESSIONAL AFFILIATIONS

Unions and professional organizations serve as forums in which ECE teachers can discuss issues related to their practice and provide support for one another. Through union membership, ECE teachers advocate their concerns about benefits through the process of collective bargaining. Under the leadership of a professional organization, for instance, ECE teachers develop position statements on professional ethics.

Research on union membership shows promising results for teacher stability. A small-scale study conducted in Washington State found that ECE teachers' union membership led to positive changes in child care centers, creating a more cooperative atmosphere in the centers and reducing annual staff turnover from 50% to 10% (Brooks, 2003). In the National Child Care Staffing Study, Whitebook and colleagues (1990) looked at unionization as one of many variables that might influence quality. The research showed that unionized teachers earned higher wages and were less likely to leave their jobs than nonunionized teachers. These findings are corroborated by a study of unionized child care programs in Canada that found unionized programs to have lower turnover rates and higher ratings on program quality scales than nonunionized programs (Doherty & Forer, 2002). Similarly, research on center-based ECE programs in Massachusetts shows that, even controlling for wages, unionized workplaces have lower turnover rates than nonunionized programs (Hatch, 2006).

Little empirical research exists on the role of professional organizations in promoting positive ECE teaching practices. Of the limited data that do exist, however, some suggest that membership is related to teacher quality and reduced turnover. McMullen and Alat (2002) studied members of the Indiana Association for the Education of Young Children (IAEYC), noting that IAEYC members were more likely to subscribe to a DAP philosophy than ECE teachers who were not members of a branch of the National Association for the Education of Young Children (NAEYC). In addition, a California-based study found that, among highly trained teachers, those who belonged to at least one professional organization were more likely to stay in their jobs (Whitebook et al., 2001).

WORK ENVIRONMENT

ECE teachers' work environment is yet another variable that affects both teacher quality and teacher effectiveness. As we use the term in this volume, *work environment* includes the physical setting, the reward system, clarity about expectations and roles, decision making, supervisor support, and communication. The physical environment, coupled with the supervision and leadership provided within it, creates the conditions under which teachers must teach. K–12 research has found that working conditions have a greater correlation with teacher turnover (and therefore, presumably, with student outcomes) than does salary (Hanushek, Kain, & Rivkin, 2001). Indeed, conditions such as school organization, teacher empowerment, instructional leadership, and facilities contribute substantially to K–12 student achievement (see, e.g., Boots, 2006; Hirsch, 2005).

Discerning the impact of the work environment on ECE teacher quality and effectiveness can be difficult and imprecise because workplace variables are defined differently in different studies. Nonetheless, some data point to correlations between work environment and teacher variables. For example, research conducted by the Child Care Services Association in North Carolina created one classification structure, identifying seven types of professional support to enhance the workplace that ECE programs can offer: (1) orientation, (2) written job descriptions, (3) written personnel policies, (4) paid education and training expenses, (5) paid breaks, (6) compensatory time for training, and (7) paid preparation/planning time. The study found that 71% of centers offered at least five of these types of support; 6% offered two or less. While 22% of teachers statewide said they would leave the field within 3 years, half as many teachers in centers offering all seven types of support said the same thing (Child Care Services Association, 2003). In Indiana, ECE teachers' satisfaction with working conditions was associated with lower levels of emotional exhaustion, a characteristic negatively associated with teacher–child interactions. This study also found that the practice of holding meetings on staff development issues was related to increased job satisfaction (Stremmel et al., 1993). These findings confirm other research that found teachers who have positive experiences in the workplace are more likely to find their jobs rewarding and remain committed to their work (Howes et al., 2003). Further, a study conducted in Australia found correlations between work environment and teacher effectiveness; a quality work environment was associated with lower levels of staff turnover, which in turn related to children's developmental outcomes (Hayden in Muijs, Aubrey, Harris, & Briggs, 2004).

Work environments affect home-based providers, as well. For FCC providers and FFN caregivers, the challenges of running a business out of the home are significant. Indeed, juggling professional roles with familial roles can be stressful for these teachers who are, literally, always at work (Nelson, 1990a). FCC providers who make a commitment to their professional work, charging higher rates and following standard business and safety practices, are more likely to be rated as sensitive, observed as responsive, and granted higher scores on an assessment of global quality (Kontos et al., 1995). These same providers are also more likely to make positive connections with other providers and remain in their positions for longer periods of time.

Supervision and Leadership

The quality of supervision and leadership provided to ECE teachers can have a great impact on teacher quality and effectiveness. Supervisors set the tone for a workplace by implementing and enforcing program policies. One study of communities in California and North Carolina examined how the quality of supervision affects the performance of teachers in child care programs serving primarily low-income communities of color (Howes et al., 2003). In this small, nonrepresentative sample, ECE teachers who were supervised in a "reflective manner" were more likely to engage in language play and responsive involvement with their students. For the purposes of this study, a reflective manner of supervision occurred when teachers met with supervisors to discuss and reflect on their practice and on the responsiveness of children to the program. It also predicted the provision of more language activities in the classroom.

Another study examined what happened in Head Start centers when their directors or lead teachers participated in the Early Childhood Leadership Training Program, a professional development program that combines graduate-level coursework and on-site technical assistance (Jorde Bloom & Sheerer, 1992). Classroom quality scores in centers where the director or lead teacher received the training were significantly higher than for classrooms where the director or teacher did not receive training. What's more, in this same study, there were positive effects on the overall organizational climate of the centers, with staff expressing more positive attitudes about the climate of, and stronger levels of commitment to, their programs after the training period. Because of the pretest–posttest methodology, these findings indicate the positive influence of leadership practices and suggest that this kind of training for directors and lead teachers can affect the quality of teaching provided by other teachers in the same program.

Accreditation

Accreditation is a process whereby center- and home-based ECE programs conduct a reflective self-analysis of their programs based on a set of quality criteria and then have their findings validated by an objective observer. If the programs achieve a specified quality standard, they receive the accreditation. Across the country, there are many different accreditation initiatives with varying degrees of stringency. Programs that achieve accreditation, however, generally are presumed to have reached a high standard of quality, as defined by the profession.

There is evidence that accreditation positively impacts program quality and teacher quality. Looking first at accreditation's effect on program quality, the National Child Care Staffing Study found that NAEYC-accredited child care centers paid higher-than-average wages and had lower teacher turnover than centers that were not accredited; both of those factors appear to contribute to teacher quality and effectiveness (Whitebook et al., 1998). An assessment of child care centers in 33 states corroborated the link between accreditation and lower levels of turnover; further, it found that accredited centers had a significantly higher quality work environment than those that were nonaccredited (Jorde-Bloom, 1996). Accredited centers allowed for more innovativeness, goal consensus, opportunities for professional growth, and clarity, and teachers at accredited centers registered higher levels of job commitment and current and desired levels of decision-making influence. One California-based study found that NAEYC-accredited centers demonstrated higher overall classroom quality than those without accreditation, but faced similar turnover rates (Whitebook, Sakai, & Howes, 1997). The discrepancy among these studies' findings on turnover may be accounted for by the indistinct correlations between turnover and compensation, work environment, and accreditation, as well as by the poorly understood nature of self-reflection inherent in the accreditation process.

Turning to the relationship between accreditation and teacher quality and effectiveness, there are somewhat mixed effects. In the same California study mentioned above, centers achieving NAEYC accreditation rated higher on measures of teacher sensitivity, but lower in terms of meeting the language-related needs of children who are English language learners, than centers that began the accreditation process but did not achieve it (Whitebook et al., 1997). In Minnesota, researchers surveyed teachers at accredited child care centers serving children of low-income families with low levels of education via a school readiness measure called the Work Sampling System Checklist (WSS), which looks at six developmental domains and measures children's ability on 32 different indicators. In comparing survey responses with statewide data (which included both accredited and nonaccredited centers), researchers found that proficiency rates were higher across all domains among the children attending accredited centers than among those in the statewide pool. Additionally, the great majority of children in accredited centers demonstrated competence in every developmental domain (Minnesota Department of Human Services, 2005).

Centers that achieve accreditation, however, do not always maintain their accreditation over time (Whitebook et al., 1998). Over a 5-year period, 60% of the NAEYC-accredited centers in the National Child Care Staffing Study lost or did not renew their accreditation. It is not known how teacher quality and effectiveness are affected when a center loses its accreditation.

CONCLUSION

In some ways, the review of the research on teacher quality and effectiveness raises more questions than it answers. In addition to glaring gaps in data germane to the ECE teaching workforce (especially FCC providers and FFN caregivers), there are limitations to generalizing any findings given that nearly all of the research cited herein was limited to small populations, specific program types, or single states. Clearly, more research is needed on the variables associated with teacher performance; for example, Tout and colleagues (2006) note that no research has examined the characteristics of teachers who are most likely to pursue professional development. The motivation teachers have to pursue education and training could very well be the same motivation that makes teachers more effective in the classroom. Similarly, there is little evidence of the threshold levels at which professional development variables do or do not have an impact on teacher quality. Stated differently, there is no certainty about the precise level of education that is most likely to enhance teacher quality and effectiveness. Further, the lack of data on child outcomes presents a severe limitation to fully understanding teacher effectiveness.

There are also a host of research questions related to the relationships among multiple variables. For example, in studying many of the correlates of teacher quality, we encounter the proverbial chicken or egg question; while the importance of wages to quality has been well documented

(Barnett, 2003b; Cost, Quality, and Child Outcomes Study Team, 1995; Lowenstein, Ochshorn, Kagan, & Fuller, 2004), we need to discern whether wages themselves attract effective teachers and improve program quality, or whether higher quality teachers are able to demand higher wages. Similarly, do enhanced and supportive workplace environments themselves improve teacher quality, or it is that higher quality teachers help to create and sustain supportive and productive workplaces?

In the debate over which factors impact teacher quality and effectiveness, some factors may be important for teachers as professionals and for the teaching workforce as a whole, even if they are not proven to be important correlates of child outcomes. For example, if research finds that no college education is necessary for teachers in order for the children they teach to have exemplary outcomes, it should not be taken to mean that ECE teachers should not pursue advanced degrees (Early et al., 2006). In fact, there may be great benefits for ECE teachers to have advanced degrees, including the ability to command higher compensation and the opportunity to move into leadership positions in the field. Teachers moving into leadership positions would strengthen the workforce as a whole, bringing to their positions the institutional and practical knowledge that they acquired in the classroom. Furthermore, there could be intergenerational benefits to ECE teachers' increased education, as it improves their own lives as well as those of the children in their classrooms and the children in their own families (Magnuson, 2002).

Given these challenges (e.g., incomplete data sets, lack of child outcome data, the chicken-egg issue), what can we say about the data? To date, three variables seem most highly predictive of teacher quality/effectiveness: (1) professional development (including formal and informal teacher education), (2) compensation, and (3) work environment. Although we are unable to speculate about the size of the effect that each has on teacher quality and effectiveness, or about the interrelationship of effects, empirical research demonstrates the positive contribution of these variables in enhancing ECE teacher quality and effectiveness. We conclude that these factors, individually and together, make a crucial difference for ECE teachers and the children they teach.

Systemic Challenges Facing
the ECE Teaching Workforce

THE DATA PRESENTED in Chapters 3 and 4 review characteristics associated with the individuals who constitute the early care and education teaching workforce. In Chapter 3, we provided a portrait of the teaching workforce, including information about their personal attributes, their professional development and experience, and their stability and compensation. In Chapter 4, we turned to data that reported on the quality and the effectiveness of ECE teachers as they carry out their jobs. We examined the differences between teacher quality and teacher effectiveness, looking at factors that are likely to influence both. Although both of these chapters focus on the individuals themselves, we know that the conditions of the ECE teaching workforce also are contoured by institutional and systemic factors. Of no small import, these factors not only provide the context within which the ECE teaching workforce functions, but also influence that context dramatically. Indeed, the ECE teaching workforce can be fully understood only through understanding the systemic contexts within which it is embedded. To that end, in this chapter we turn to a discussion of two overarching challenges that subsume and profoundly affect the ECE teaching workforce. First, the ECE teaching workforce is rooted in the nascent, struggling ECE system—a system that has long been characterized as a "non-system" because of its vast array of uncoordinated programs and policies and its lack of an essential infrastructure. Second, the ECE workforce in the United States operates within a market-based economy characterized by imperfections and incompleteness. This chapter reviews these two broad challenges, highlighting particular challenges they evoke for the ECE teaching workforce in the form of professional development infrastructure and compensation.

THE ECE NON-SYSTEM: MULTIPLE POLICIES AND PROGRAMS
WITH INADEQUATE INFRASTRUCTURE

Often described as a non-system with disparate funding streams, eligibility requirements, program quality standards, teacher qualifications, and governance structures, ECE in the United States is a hybrid of programs and policies that have emerged over decades, with little coherent policy planning and even less organization. Some programs arose to meet the needs of children of the indigent; other programs were created to meet the needs of working parents; still other programs were established to provide part-time, education-focused experiences for young children. This historic programmatic orientation of ECE has led to the emergence of a complex array of public and private, center-based and home-based, and for-profit and not-for-profit microenterprises. Some programs are subsidized by the government while others depend solely on parental tuition, with many programs having a blend of public and private funding sources. Nonprofit programs may function as independent organizations with their own 501(c)3 status, or they may be run as part of larger organizations, such as religious, community-based, and civic institutions (e.g., United Way).

Not merely an artifact of happenstance, this cacophony of programs has been institutionalized in policy. At the federal level, for example, there are scores of programs for young children, including the Child Care and Development Fund (CCDF), Head Start and Early Head Start, and programs for children with disabilities. First, CCDF is administered by the U.S. Department of Health and Human Services' (HHS) Child Care Bureau and is focused primarily on providing child care supports to families currently dependent on cash benefits, and on preventing other families from falling into welfare dependency. States receive this funding in the form of a block grant that provides subsidies for low-income families. Although the CCDF legislation does not make specific provisions for ECE teachers' qualifications and professional development, states establish their own child care regulations that address these issues, and, as will be detailed in Chapter 6, they vary widely. The federal CCDF legislation does require each state to set aside a minimum of 4% of its CCDF block grant funding to improve the quality and accessibility of child care (Pittard, Zaslow, Lavelle, & Porter, 2006). Using these funds, states and localities have pursued many innovative strategies to enhance the ECE workforce, including many of the policies and programs discussed in Part III of this volume.

Head Start and Early Head Start, the second major federal ECE effort, also are administered by HHS and provide comprehensive child development and family support programs for very low-income families. Head Start serves children of preschool age (3- and 4-year-olds) and Early Head Start serves low-income families with infants and toddlers, as well as women who are pregnant. Both programs provide an array of child and family services, including family support, parenting education, self-sufficiency support, and early childhood development programs. With the reauthorization of Head

Start in 1998, the federal government increased the professional requirements for Head Start teachers so that at least 50% of all Head Start teachers would have an associate's degree or higher in early childhood education or a related field by 2003. Head Start's reauthorization—due in 2003, but still pending in Congress as of mid-2007—will likely raise these requirements. To support professional development, Head Start dedicates resources to quality improvement, which programs use to improve teachers' qualifications, training, and salaries (Welch-Ross, Wolf, Moorehouse, & Rathgeb, 2006).

Third, the federal government supports ECE programs through various initiatives of the U.S. Department of Education, including the Individuals with Disabilities Education Act (IDEA), a significant effort that serves young children in diverse settings. In addition, Title I of No Child Left Behind (NCLB) funds compensatory education for disadvantaged students and may be used both to provide stand-alone preschool programs and to supplement or expand other early care and education programs, such as Head Start. Any preschool program funded by Title I must meet Head Start's quality performance standards and, in cases where preschool is "part of (the state's) elementary and secondary school system," preschool teachers must meet the state's NCLB "highly qualified" teacher provisions (Ewan & Matthews, 2006).

Adding complexity to the ECE programmatic landscape, most states and many localities also fund programs and services for young children. Although there are a few places with long histories of involvement and investment in ECE, the most prolific increase in state and local involvement has occurred over the past 2 decades. Some states fund prekindergarten programs; others invest state funds in Head Start; others contribute funding to improve child care quality; still others provide ECE-related tax benefits directly to parents. States vary not only with regard to the qualifications they require for teachers, but also with regard to how they elect to invest resources. Taking only one program type as an example, state-funded pre-kindergarten, New Jersey expends $9,854 per enrolled child, while South Carolina spends $1,085 per enrolled child (Barnett et al., 2006).

An Emerging ECE System and the Centrality of the Workforce

Recognizing that ECE is not functioning as an integrated whole, but as a set of highly idiosyncratic and uncoordinated arrangements, policymakers, researchers, and practitioners have begun to consider the desirability and feasibility of creating a more integrated system. To help advance a system-based agenda, many scholars have defined what constitutes a fully functioning ECE system (Bruner, 2004; Gallagher, Clifford, & Maxwell, 2004;

Kagan & Cohen, 1997; Kagan & Rigby, 2003). Although there is some variation among these scholars, most agree that a system must have multiple components that are well synchronized. Early definitions of a system suggested that it has two essential parts: first, the programs and direct services children receive, and second, the infrastructure that supports the programs (Kagan & Cohen, 1997). In this rendering, the infrastructure includes the supports that perform a specialized or essential function for the whole system (e.g., regulation, finance, governance, workforce development, quality assurance mechanisms). Transcending any single program, a strong infrastructure binds together traditionally disparate programs and services by providing common standards, reliable funding, and sensible oversight. As a result, a focus on the infrastructure would help eliminate the inequities that traditionally have characterized American ECE.

As noted, even though there is some variation in the precise components of an ECE system proffered by various scholars, every definition of the infrastructure, irrespective of author, includes workforce development. While some suggest that workforce development is the nucleus of a system, all acknowledge that the workforce development infrastructure faces many challenges because, like the individuals and programs they serve, workforce supports are diverse and often underresourced. The ECE teaching workforce, in particular, faces multiple challenges, including the lack of systematization across institutions of higher education (IHEs), as well as the lack of systematization among community-based training providers, low or nonexistent professional development requirements, inconsistent career ladders for ECE teachers, insufficient leadership development for ECE program directors, inadequate coursework and experiences that reflect the growing diversity of America's children and families, inconsistent databases for tracking both education and training opportunities and teachers' professional development, and no standard evaluation models (Smith, Sarkar, Perry-Manning, & Schmalzried, 2006). Throughout this volume, evidence of these challenges—and, in many instances, evidence of innovative efforts to redress them—is abundant. To illustrate in more depth the impact of the lack of a system on the ECE workforce, we turn to an examination of professional development, specifically (1) the people who educate and train ECE teachers (i.e., teacher educators and teacher trainers), and (2) the content of the formal education and training provided (i.e., the curriculum, coursework, and experiences).

Inadequate Systematization of ECE Teacher Educators and Trainers

Just as the effectiveness of the ECE teaching workforce determines the quality of child outcomes, the effectiveness of those who educate ECE teachers determines whether or not those teachers are prepared to make many of the positive impacts described in Chapter 4. Unfortunately, there has been little systemization of the qualifications and experiences required of faculty members who prepare ECE teachers in 2- and 4-year institutions of higher education and those who facilitate ongoing training and other professional development efforts. In many respects, it will be difficult to raise the quality of the ECE teaching workforce until teacher educators and teacher trainers are more capable of providing the kind of professional development that prepares high-quality ECE teachers.

In formal education, ECE teacher educators—faculty members at 2- and 4-year institutions of higher education—have varying levels of education, leading to great disparities in the depth of their knowledge and quality of their own teaching. In a nationally representative survey of 1,179 heads of early childhood teacher preparation programs at 2- and 4-year IHEs, the National Prekindergarten Center at the Frank Porter Graham Child Development Institute found that, while 45% of ECE faculty at 4-year institutions had an MA and 53% of ECE faculty had a doctoral degree, 76% of ECE faculty at 2-year institutions had an MA and just 8% held a doctoral degree (Maxwell, Lim, & Early, 2006). Furthermore, among all degree-holding ECE faculty, just 45% at 4-year institutions and 61% at 2-year institutions had degrees in early childhood that specifically pertained to children from birth to age 4. ECE faculty also differed according to their levels of firsthand experience working with young children in ECE programs. According to the same study, 75% of ECE faculty had direct experience working with young children, but a significantly smaller percentage of faculty at 4-year institutions had such experience as compared with faculty at 2-year institutions—64% versus 84%.

Even when ECE faculty are well educated and have extensive field experience, there simply are not enough of them to adequately educate and prepare ECE teachers. In California, for example, ECE preparation programs employ fewer full-time faculty and have worse faculty to student ratios than other academic programs (Whitebook, Bellm, Lee, & Sakai, 2005). Indeed, the problem of high faculty to student ratios persists across the country: In 1999, the mean number of students per full-time faculty member across 438 institutions of higher education was 39; in early childhood teacher preparation programs at those same institutions, the ratio was 61:1 (Early & Winton, 2001).

Outside of formal education, in the realm of community-based professional development and training, the most recent and comprehensive review of ECE training programs comes from a survey by the National Association of Child Care Resource and Referral Agencies (NACCRRA) of 18 state networks of child care resource and referral agencies (CCR&Rs),

as well as a random, representative sample of 169 local CCR&Rs and three CCR&Rs that serve entire states (Smith et al., 2006). Among local CCR&Rs that provide training, 76% of staff who actually deliver training to ECE teachers had a bachelor's degree or higher, and 18% had an associate's degree; 44% of all trainers' college-level degrees were specifically in the field of early childhood (Smith et al., 2006).

Inadequate Systematization of the Content of ECE Teacher Preparation

Beyond the quality and background of ECE faculty and trainers themselves, the content of the curriculum and experiences that they offer to ECE teachers has a significant impact on the quality and effectiveness of ECE teachers. According to available data, the content of most teacher training programs in 2- and 4-year institutions of higher education is too limited to prepare students for the diversity of demands they will face as ECE teachers.

In terms of the content of formal education, while the large majority of ECE teacher preparation programs across the country require one or more courses on the education and care of young children, 22% of BA programs and 16% of AA programs do not require a full course (Maxwell, Lim, & Early, 2006) on this most basic and essential subject (Hutchinson, 1994; Kramer, 1994; Lobman et al., 2005; Pianta, 2007; Rowe et al., 1994). Furthermore, in terms of preparing all ECE teachers to understand the development and learning of very young children, in 2004, 50% of BA programs and 28% of AA programs did not require a full course on the education and care of infants and toddlers; however, these percentages had improved from 60% of BA programs and 40% of AA programs in 1999 (Early & Winton, 2001; Maxwell et al., 2006), suggesting that ECE teacher preparation programs may be responding to the increasing number of very young children in early care and education. Furthermore, even when offered, this content may be limited in particularly detrimental ways. As Ray, Bowman, and Robbins (2006) write, "Perhaps 75% of the professional curriculum in bachelor's degree teacher education programs is primarily concerned with the development and education of white middle class, able bodied, monolingual children" (p. 36). They add "The developmental and educational needs of *all* children simply *do not* appear to be at the center of teacher preparation coursework and practice" (p. 39; emphasis in original). Further illuminating the limited curricular content of formal education, most ECE teacher preparation programs do not prepare teachers to work in the great variety of environments that characterize the ECE field. For example, 95% of BA programs and 88% of AA programs in a national sample did not require a full course on working in family child care homes (Early & Winton, 2001).

Even when these topics are embraced by a wide variety of teacher preparation programs, the absence of standardized coursework yields considerable variation. Isenberg (2000) argues that the precise knowledge base of child development—by far the most often included subject in ECE teacher preparation programs—remains disputed. Furthermore, Isenberg identifies a particular shortcoming facing current teacher preparation programs: an overemphasis on developmental knowledge that remains disconnected from curriculum preparation. Indeed, examining existing empirical analyses of the NICHD Study of Early Child Care and Youth Development, the state prekindergarten study conducted by the National Center for Early Development and Learning, and the Early Childhood Longitudinal Study–Kindergarten Cohort, Pianta (2007) concludes that "the evidence is quite clear that it is the teacher's *implementation* of a curriculum, through both social and instructional interactions with children, that produces effects on students learning" (p. 46; emphasis in original). Therefore, curricular implementation linked to developmental theory may be the most important and underrepresented areas of existing teacher preparation coursework (Fein, 1994; Lobman et al., 2005).

Finally, too many ECE teacher preparation programs still do not require all of their students to complete practica, which professional development experts agree are crucial to high-quality teacher training programs (Fein, 1994; Lobman et al., 2005; Pianta, 2007). While nearly all associate's and bachelor's degree programs nationally require practica for future teachers of 3- and 4-year-olds (Maxwell, Lim, & Early, 2006), just two-thirds require practica for students who intend to work with infants and toddlers (children under the age of 3), and less than 10% require practica for students planning to work in FCC homes (Early & Winton, 2001; Maxwell et al., 2006). Similarly, among California's ECE teacher preparation programs, only associate's degree programs commonly require practica; just 15% of bachelor's degree and 7% of master's level programs require teaching experience for graduation (Whitebook et al., 2005). Given the value of contact with children and experienced teachers, the surprising scarcity of practicum requirements represents yet another challenge to the establishment of high-quality ECE teacher preparation programs.

As this discussion suggests, the lack of a system for preparing ECE teachers is apparent not only in the qualifications of ECE teacher educators and trainers, but also in the content of that preparation. At once, this lack of a system of ECE teacher preparation reflects and affects challenges facing American early care and education. That there is no systematic approach to teaching workforce preparation should not surprise us, given the lack of any system of ECE. The question at hand is why there is not an

ECE system in the United States. To further address this complex issue, we turn to a discussion of the unique market system of American ECE, the second of our two major contextual challenges.

ECE AS AN INCOMPLETE MARKET

American ECE is a market hallmarked by a paradox: It renders both a public and a private good. As Warner and colleagues (2004) have pointed out, ECE is a private good in that it allows parents to work; it is a public good in that it prepares children for school, enhances the productivity of schools, and ultimately increases the economic capacity of society. As a public and a private good, early care and education services are funded and delivered by government-sponsored agencies, private community-based organizations, and individual business owners and entrepreneurs, with many private-sector ECE programs accepting public dollars. Early care and education is not alone in facing this paradox; indeed, as public goods and services become privatized and private services become increasingly publicly subsidized, the lines that once segregated public and private sectors are blurred (Salamon, 2002).

The blurring of the sectors denotes shifts and differences in markets and in the way in which they perform. We know, for example, that coordinated markets (e.g., continental Europe) are characterized by high job protection, long tenure in positions, considerable industry (or firm-specific) training, and extensive labor coordination and bargaining. Thus, coordinated market economies protect workers' investment in their own skill development. By contrast, American early care and education can be regarded as a private liberal market economy wherein consumer choice is the driving force (Adema, 2001; Hacker, 2003). Liberal market economies are often somewhat deregulated; workers lack protections and generous benefits, and turnover is typically high (Hall & Soskice, 2001). Not all services in a liberal market economy are subject to these characteristics; many K–12 teachers in the United States, for example, are protected by unions that set compensation levels to protect teachers' extensive investments in their professional preparation (Morgan, 2005).

Those who characterize ECE as part of a private liberal market economy do so because most direct public subsidies are limited to low-income families through the tax code, cash subsidies, and various regulatory provisions. Increasingly, however, ECE is recognized as a public good, with services being made available to increasing numbers of children, regardless of family income. Indeed, reflecting an ideological shift away from devoting public funds only to low-income families, some recent policies, including burgeoning investments in state-funded prekindergarten and changes in certain tax policies, funnel funds to families with diverse incomes.

Resting on highly publicized results from effective early childhood interventions, as well as the bevy of brain development studies that attest to children's early intellectual capacity, many policymakers and other leaders no longer consider ECE as babysitting or for children from low-income families alone; instead, it has become the first stage in a formal education system (Peters & Bristow, 2006). Indeed, in the recent report *Tough Choices or Tough Times* (New Commission on the Skills of the American Workforce, 2007), early care and education was heralded as a necessity for all 4-year-old children and an essential component of a reformed educational system. As such, ECE increasingly is considered a necessary public good, essential to the overall well-being of the nation.

Whether ECE is a public or private good, and whether we want to see greater public investments in ECE, is open to debate. What is not debated is that the "market" in which ECE operates is subject to market forces (e.g., price, convenience, perceived quality). Some would suggest that the market is "underdeveloped" (Warner et al., 2004). Others would say that the market is subject to market failure (Hansmann, 1980). Whichever terminology one uses, contemporary ECE needs to be understood as a market that is compromised. Often, compromised markets are characterized by low entry requirements for workers, low wages, limited economies of scale, inefficient product differentiation by consumers, imperfect consumer knowledge, and limited protections. In the case of ECE, the market is further compromised because it is an industry in which direct consumers (children) have no voice.

Scholars have examined the performance of markets in order to explain why they fail. Walker (1995), for example, notes that noncompetitive behavior, imperfect information, and incomplete markets lead to market failure. Noncompetitive behavior occurs when a firm is able to affect the market price because it grows large enough to create a monopoly, thereby rendering the market noncompetitive. While there are not monopolies in ECE, noncompetition exists because, although parents ostensibly have choice, in reality many parents do not. Choice is constrained by the cost of the programs, by most parents' inability or unwillingness to transport young children for long distances or long hours on a daily basis, and by the availability (or lack thereof) of ECE options in certain communities. Next, imperfect information exists in ECE because parents often are unable to discern what constitutes quality or because their definition of quality may vary from a professional standard. Variables not related to quality (e.g., location, hours, and dependability) exert powerful influences upon choice, rendering the use of information about quality (e.g., teacher qualifications, classroom environment), if information exists, less potent. Finally, incomplete markets occur when individuals are unable to exchange goods at a given price in a given time period (Warner et al., 2004). Consider the example of a woman entering the labor force who has found child care. If the woman is unsure of the length of her employment, she will be unable to predict her future demand for ECE and will be unwilling to pay up front for future care. As a result, the ECE program operator cannot depend on the woman for ongoing income, and the operator's market is incomplete. Externalities, such as the opening of a publicly funded pre-kindergarten, also limit predictability of use over time and fuel incomplete markets. The existence of market failure in ECE helps to explain why change in the field has been slow and difficult.

Another characteristic of compromised markets is market spillover. Spillover occurs when an intervention impacts outcomes beyond those directly targeted (Peters & Bristow, 2006). Examples of market spillover include a reduction in the supply of ECE when regulations are enhanced; because regulations increase minimum licensing requirements and involve greater expenditures (e.g., for increased training and improved ratios), they raise costs. For ECE programs, this means that profits are harder to realize, resulting in increased costs for parents, who may elect to withdraw children from programs. Reduced demand, in turn, forces programs to reduce supply. Without intending to, regulations impact supply.

Spillover also occurs when something happens in an allied field that impacts ECE teachers. When changes in Medicaid rules caused a greater demand for nursing home aides, for example, many ECE teachers who were in assistant or aide positions left the field to obtain higher wages offered by nursing homes. Market interactions, then, occur within the ECE field itself and beyond, and they must be considered when creating recommendations for the ECE teaching workforce.

As the above examples indicate, the ECE workforce's position within a failed market dramatically impacts teachers' compensation. The central challenge in the flailing ECE market has been identified as a tug-of-war among three competing factors: program and service quality, affordability for parents, and compensation for ECE teachers (Mitchell, Stoney, & Dichter, 2001). Pulling on or increasing any one aspect of this triad can have serious financial impact on the other aspects. For example, increasing teachers' compensation without infusing the system with substantial amounts of new resources from either government or business may make ECE programs entirely unaffordable for many families.

Furthermore, because parents have imperfect information, they may not be able to discern between more and less competent teachers and, therefore, they may not be able to weigh the costs and benefits of paying higher prices for the services. Without parent demand for teachers with higher qualifications, the need for better qualified and higher compensated teachers diminishes (from the market perspective). Lacking the incentive of higher compensation, ECE teachers are less interested in pursuing more training, furthering a cycle of low qualifications and low compensation. If the market was not compromised, teachers would have greater incentive to pursue more professional development, which, in turn, could evoke higher compensation.

When programs expand and entry gates to the market are lowered so that programs will have sufficient staff, the opportunity for increased compensation withers. Without consistent entry requirements, the market is open to all potential workers who meet minimal qualifications; as a result, the supply of workers expands. When the supply of workers in the labor pool is large and consumers (parents) cannot recognize quality, employers have no financial incentive to hire workers with higher levels of professional preparation; as a result of this, compensation drops. Increasingly, as both private and public ECE programs expand, compensation needs to be adjusted so that equity prevails and turnover is staved.

To date, ECE teachers actually subsidize the market because of their forgone wages. Forgone wages are the difference between the wages a teacher actually receives and the wages she could earn in other occupations that require similar qualifications. While some ECE workers select the field as a place of employment because of nonmonetary benefits (e.g., working with children, being close to home, or desirable hours) and, thus, willingly forgo appropriate wages, most do not.

Returning to the tug-of-war analogy, if parents lack the information or the ability to pay more for ECE services, and if teachers are already forgoing wages to subsidize the market, one obvious solution would be to infuse greater amounts of government funding—or subsidies from corporate America—to increase teachers' compensation. To this, though, Peters and Bristow (2006) offer a warning. They contend that the provision of subsidies to improve the qualifications of ECE teachers ultimately may depress, rather than increase, wages. They reason that if teachers receive more training, they will be able to earn higher wages. As the supply of these trained workers increases, however, they will become less scarce, so the wages they can command will be lower. In the short run, these effects will be less apparent than in the long run. They also will be less apparent if other markets for the trained workers (e.g., the public schools) are increasingly available. Peters and Bristow (2006) also suggest that any analysis of increased publicly subsidized professional development should take into consideration the increased taxes that will be needed to fund the efforts. If the cost of increased wages results in much higher taxation for

the newly trained teacher, then the incentives for such training are reduced, as is the impact of professional development on teachers' income.

Despite these warnings, there is no question that compensation is critical
to sustaining a qualified workforce. Given an imperfect market, however,
the avenues for increasing compensation, while varied, are problematic.
Public subsidies in the form of new public investments can be made, given
adequate political and public will; doing so, however, increasingly will push
ECE into a controlled market. Alternatively, fees from parents can be increased (although many parents will be unable to afford increased fees), a
strategy that will reinforce the mixed market. Less desirably, ECE teachers can continue to subsidize the field via their forgone wages (a decid-
edly inequitable strategy that will perpetuate extant challenges). Given
these situations, Folbre's (2006) sentiment for change should be seriously
considered: "You don't need to obey the laws of supply and demand if they
are not working; you need to write new laws" (p. 26).

CONCLUSION

The intention of this chapter has been to suggest that the ECE teaching
workforce not only is composed of individuals, but is shaped by contextual and institutional irregularities. American ECE functions at multiple
levels (federal, state, and local), as a component of a non-system of ECE
services that includes direct programs and infrastructure, and as part of
an imperfect ECE market.

Yet, armed with a new understanding of the importance of ECE as a
market, and an imperfect one at that, new improvement efforts are emerging. For example, policies and programs have recognized that professional
development and incentives to inspire it are critical. Efforts to improve
workforce capacity are no longer conceptualized as isolated undertakings,
but as part of broader and more systemic quality enhancements. Funding, which had once been devoted exclusively to supporting direct services
for children, is now being devoted also to supporting the infrastructure.
The idea, but not the reality, of an ECE system has taken hold within the
ECE field.

The Political and Public Will: What Is Currently Being Done?

IN ACCORDANCE with Julius Richmond's model of social change, Part II provided an overview of the existing knowledge base related to the early care and education teaching workforce. Part III outlines efforts to improve the ECE teaching workforce and the ECE system in the United States, providing evidence of the political and public will, nascent though they are, supporting the ECE workforce. Richmond defined political will as "society's desire and commitment to support or modify old programs or to develop new programs" (Richmond & Kotelchuck, 1984, p. 207). To the extent that the policies and programs discussed in the next three chapters required public resources, they represent public will. Given, though, that none of the policies or programs have been taken to scale across the nation, we assert that the political and public will for ECE workforce reform is both emergent and fragile.

This is not to suggest that there are few efforts to improve the ECE teaching workforce. On the contrary, there are many such efforts—so many, in fact, they could not all be included here. To illustrate the scope of workforce improvement initiatives, we include evaluated efforts where possible and present a rich array of policies and programs from across the country and, in a few cases, around the world. This array highlights important work at federal, state, county, and community levels. Efforts described herein directly address at least one of the three main factors related to ECE teacher quality reported in Chapter 4 (professional development, compensation, and work environment); as a compendium, these policies and programs impact diverse populations of ECE teachers and rely on diverse service delivery systems. The result is a wide range of initiatives, conveying a broad scope of effort.

In order to better understand the diverse ECE workforce initiatives, we have developed a three-tier typology (see accompanying illustration). At the apex of the pyramid are those efforts with the most narrow or targeted missions. The designation of efforts as having targeted missions is a descriptive, not an evaluative, label. Rich in texture and depth, the first tier encompasses efforts that: (a) focus on enhancing professional development; (b) seek to increase compensation; and (c) improve teachers' work

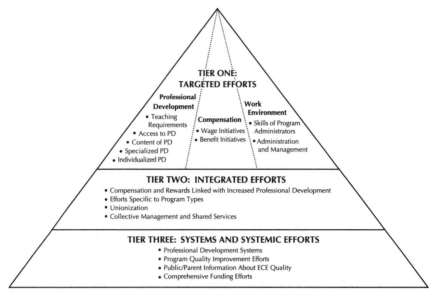

A conceptual model for ECE teaching workforce policies and programs.

environments. Discussed in Chapter 6, each of the three types represents one of the predictors of teacher quality and effectiveness evoked from our review of the knowledge base.

The second tier of the pyramid, discussed in Chapter 7, includes efforts with integrated missions; in general, these policies and programs seek to achieve multiple goals concurrently. They recognize that the challenges facing ECE teachers are highly interrelated, and, therefore, they offer multifaceted solutions. The second tier includes efforts that, for example, aim to improve teachers' educational attainment *and* compensation *and* stability. Also included are policies specific to a program type (e.g., those of Head Start) that not only provide incentives for ECE teachers to improve their professional qualifications, but also offer higher compensation in return for those improvements.

At the base of the pyramid, the third tier, discussed in Chapter 8, encompasses systemic efforts with the broadest and most comprehensive missions. Included here are professional development systems and initiatives that promote greater coordination among diverse ECE programs, professional development institutions, and workforce-related policies. Policies and programs that transcend the ECE workforce and address other components of an ECE infrastructure (e.g., public awareness, overall public and private investments in ECE) also are included. Because these types of efforts are the most comprehensive, they form the broadest part of the pyramid, its base.

Although plentiful, the efforts reviewed in Chapters 6, 7, and 8 reflect the diffuse development of political and public will in some places and among some policymakers and leaders. Existing ECE teaching workforce reform efforts also reflect the dedication and tenacity of the ECE field itself. Recognition of the importance of the teaching workforce and its place at the fulcrum of high-quality ECE exists in some measure, but has not yet grown to reflect the political and public will of an entire nation. The policies and programs presented herein are both a tribute to the work accomplished to date and a beacon for what could be accomplished for all, given increased political and public support for and attention to ECE workforce issues.

CHAPTER 6

Tier One: Targeted Efforts

EVIDENCE OF the political and public commitment to improving the ECE workforce can be found in the many policies and programs launched across the United States to address specific challenges. These policies and programs have highly targeted missions often motivated by the research and knowledge base presented in Part II, which indicates that children benefit from teachers who (1) have professional development that involves both formal education and training, especially with specialized focus on child development and early care and education; (2) are well compensated; and/or (3) work in supportive and professional environments. Independently, each of these three factors increases workforce stability and improves teacher quality and effectiveness; collectively, they form the top tier of the pyramid and are discussed, in turn, below.

EFFORTS TO IMPROVE PROFESSIONAL DEVELOPMENT

Throughout the nation, many efforts designed to improve professional development have been launched. Because there are many different kinds of initiatives, we have classified them as efforts to (1) improve teaching requirements, (2) increase access to professional development opportunities, (3) enhance the content of professional development offerings, (4) support specialized professional development that addresses current and emerging needs in the field, and (5) provide one-on-one interactions for teachers to enhance their teaching competencies. Examples of each of these efforts are presented below.

Improving Teaching Requirements

The first and most ubiquitous strategy to enhance professional development is not a programmatic strategy, but policy-based strategies that regulate who is permitted to teach. Throughout the nation, states have implemented program regulations that govern which programs can operate legally. In many cases, these regulations also stipulate the minimum requirements for individuals to become (entry requirements) and to remain (ongoing requirements) a teacher. Even though there is considerable variation among states in what is required (LeMoine & Azer, 2006a, 2006b), studies attest to the influence of regulatory policies in improving the quality of ECE (Helburn, 1995; Phillips et al., 2001).

Entry Requirements. Entry requirements form the basic minimum expectations for those entering the ECE teaching workforce; as such, they can be a potent tool for quality enhancement. States vary, however, with regard to whether they have entry requirements and, for those states that have them, the level at which they are set and the population to which they apply also vary considerably. As of 2006, 38 states had no minimum entry requirements in ECE for teachers in licensed child care programs. Of the twelve states that require teachers to have minimum education or training in early childhood development, two require a Child Development Associate (CDA) or Child Care Provider (CCP) credential, four require a credential plus experience, two require the completion of a vocational child care program, and four require some mix of education and training or training and experience (LeMoine & Azer, 2006a). Where they exist, these entry requirements typically apply to all teachers working in all licensed child care centers. FCC providers face less stringent requirements than ECE teachers in center-based programs; only 14 states require FCC teachers to meet ECE entry requirements, which range from specified hours of training and years of experience to satisfactory performance on competency exams and CDA credentialing (LeMoine & Azer, 2006b). Even though FFN caregivers are exempt from licensing, those receiving child care subsidies are subject to some entry requirements. States, for example, may require FFN caregivers to undergo a background check and/or home inspection, to sign and submit a self-certification, or to participate in an orientation and training. In fact, 15 states require FFN caregivers to participate in training that addresses health, safety, and, in two of those states, child development (Porter & Kearns, 2005).

Typically, entry requirements for teachers in both the federal Head Start program and state-funded prekindergarten programs are more stringent than for those in child care. Looking first at Head Start, in 1998, Congress required 50% of Head Start teachers across the nation to hold associate's degrees by 2003. As of 2005, 33% had associate's, 31% had bachelor's, and 5% had graduate degrees; in total, 19% more Head Start teachers held advanced degrees than was mandated by the federal government (Hamm, 2006). These data reinforce the fact that most entry requirements are set at minimum, not maximum, required levels. As a result, even though policy may establish a minimum level for teacher qualifications, many programs and providers exceed that standard.

Turning to state-funded prekindergarten, of the 52 programs across the nation (some states have more than one prekindergarten program), 21 require prekindergarten teachers to have bachelor's degrees (of which 16 also require a teaching certificate), 20 require them to have CDAs, and three require them to have associate's degrees in early childhood education (Gilliam & Marchesseault, 2005). Only eight programs have no minimum entry requirements. A potent example of the role that state regulation plays in increasing teachers' qualifications can be seen in the 2000 New Jersey Supreme Court decision in *Abbott* v. *Burke,* which mandated that the poorest urban school districts in the state provide high-quality preschool for all 3- and 4-year-old children. *Abbott* required that all ECE teachers in the state-funded prekindergarten program earn bachelor's degrees and P–3 (preschool through grade 3) certificates by September 2004 (Coffman & Lopez, 2003); from 2000 to 2004, the percentage of teachers in *Abbott* districts in compliance with the mandate jumped from 35% to 82.2%, and most of the remaining teachers were pursuing bachelor's degrees or certification (Ryan & Ackerman, 2005).

To put ECE teachers' entry requirements in context, it is helpful to consider states' entry requirements for K–12 teachers. All 50 states require the vast majority of K–12 teachers to obtain teaching credentials prior to becoming licensed. Within each state, the requirements for those teaching the same grades and/or subjects are fairly consistent, irrespective of school or district. To achieve the requirements, teachers must have a bachelor's degree and also must complete an approved formal teacher education program that typically includes a specified number of credits, subject-area coursework, and supervised practice teaching (Bureau of Labor Statistics, 2006b). Most states also require K–12 teachers to pass a certification exam that assesses their skills and knowledge. Within these K–12 regulations, there is some variation across states, yet this variation pales in comparison to the diversity of entry requirements that characterizes ECE.

Ongoing Requirements. Many states have focused on enhancing the training requirements for ECE teachers already employed in the field. Ongoing professional development supports teachers as they employ effective teaching practices that reflect both current pedagogical strategies and up-to-date knowledge about children's development and learning. For center-based ECE teachers, these requirements vary from state to state, with only four states *not* requiring any ongoing training or education. Twenty-three states require between 1 and 12 hours of annual training, twelve states require an average of 13 to 19 hours, and nine states require more than

19 hours of ongoing training per year; two states and the District of Columbia require an unspecified amount of training (LeMoine & Azer, 2006a).

States also set—and have been increasing—ongoing professional development requirements for FCC providers. In 1986, only eight states required any ongoing training for FCC providers; in 2006, 36 states required FCC providers to participate in some form of ongoing training, but no state yet includes formal education among the ongoing requirements for FCC providers. Of these thirty-six states, twenty-seven require an average of 1 to 12 hours of annual training, five require an average of 13 to 19 hours annually, and two require more than 19 hours of training per year; additionally, two states mandate unspecified hours of ongoing training (LeMoine & Azer, 2006b).

Increasing Access to Professional Development

The second type of effort used to enhance ECE teachers' professional development consists of increasing their access to it. Initiatives to increase teachers' access to professional development take three primary forms: using technology, providing financial assistance, and making the transfer of credit easier through articulation agreements.

ECE teachers, as adult learners who often have full-time jobs and family responsibilities, face many barriers to accessing meaningful professional development opportunities. Professional development opportunities may not be in geographic proximity to ECE teachers, making access logistically difficult. In addition, because teachers receive little or no financial return on their investment in additional training, the personal costs of pursuing professional development often far outweigh the benefits (Mitchell & Morgan, 2000). Furthermore, college may be an unfamiliar or daunting environment for ECE teachers who wish to (or must) pursue credentials or degrees offered in institutions of higher education. Therefore, expanding access to professional development opportunities is crucial for teachers' practice and sense of professional worth, as well as for child outcomes.

Technology-Mediated Learning. Technology-mediated learning is an umbrella term encompassing an approach to professional development that takes place exclusively via the Internet (e.g., distance learning, online learning, web-based learning, and e-learning) and professional development that combines interaction between students and instructors with content delivered via the Internet and other technology-based modes of communication (e.g., satellite training). Such professional development opportunities break down long-standing boundaries of location (e.g., by allowing someone in Hawaii to take a course, or even earn a degree, offered in Minnesota) and time (e.g., by helping someone at work from 7:00 in the morning to 6:00 in the evening attend courses typically offered during the afternoon). While relevant to all ECE teachers, technology has the potential to overcome the logistical access barriers to professional development facing FCC providers, who typically work longer hours, have more constraints on their daily schedules, and are more isolated than center-based teachers. Although Western Governors University received NCATE accreditation for its online program to license prekindergarten teachers and English language learning specialists (Keller, 2006), there are not yet widely accepted means to ensure the content and pedagogical quality of technology-mediated learning.

According to the National Child Care Information Center (NCCIC), technology-mediated learning efforts exist in more than 20 states (National Child Care Information Center, 2004). ECE teachers in Oklahoma, for example, can access the state's mandated entry-level child care training online. Because Oklahoma's center licensing regulations require all entry-level teachers to complete this training within the first 90 days of employment, this innovative effort successfully integrates technology-mediated learning into the state's core licensing regulations. As another example, the University of Alaska offers a distance-delivered associate's degree in ECE to rural Alaskan students via audio-conference, e-mail, fax, and computer conferencing. In a state with a widely dispersed population and many remote communities, this is an important effort for providing professional development to ECE teachers who otherwise may be geographically isolated from formal education and training. In addition, organizations such as the National Head Start Association and institutions of higher education (IHEs) such as Concordia University in St. Paul, Minnesota, provide distance learning to individuals across the country.

Additional interactive technological innovations, such as video-conferencing and training modules on videotape and CD-ROM, have introduced new methods of preparing ECE teachers, breaking the traditional time and space boundaries of classroom observations and detailed instructor feedback. The MyTeachingPartner project, for example, enables consultants to observe teachers interacting with young children in the classroom. In this way, technology facilitates individualized guidance that traditionally has been confined to student-teachers in lab school settings (Pianta, 2006).

Financial Assistance. A second approach to increasing teachers' access to professional development is through financial incentives. Because so many ECE teachers are poorly paid, spending portions of their very limited personal resources on professional development often is not a re-alistic option. Consequently, the provision of financial assistance can mean-ingfully enhance ECE teachers' desire for and access to formal education and training. There are two predominant targeted strategies for enhanc-ing financial access to professional development: loan forgiveness efforts and reimbursements for education and training. Programs like T.E.A.C.H. Early Childhood®, which offer scholarships in combination with other workforce supports, are addressed later in this book.

Loan forgiveness programs cancel all or part of an educational loan, provided the loan recipient (here, the ECE teacher) fulfills certain work-related requirements. Such programs have been implemented by the fed-eral government and in several states. In 2001, the federal government initiated the Federal Child Care Providers Loan Forgiveness demonstra-tion project. To be eligible, ECE teachers had to have (1) received an associate's or bachelor's degree in the field of early childhood education, and (2) provided full-time care to low-income children for the 2 consecu-tive years preceding the year in which forgiveness was requested. A per-centage of a borrower's loan was forgiven for each year the teacher provided child care in a low-income community, reaching 100% forgiveness after 5 consecutive years (Federal Student Aid, 2002). Unfortunately, funding for this program was not renewed in 2004 (Child Care Bureau, 2004a). In 2000, the Colorado General Assembly launched a similar effort with its Colorado Early Childhood Professional Loan Repayment Program. Upon graduation with an associate's degree, teachers who work in a licensed child care program are eligible for a loan repayment of $1,000 (College Invest, n.d.). This program, however, currently is threatened because of underutilization; the professional development community is trying to publicize this benefit to increase participation (K. Stiles, personal commu-nication, May 14, 2007). Colorado's experience suggests that ECE teach-ers need support and outreach to participate in loan forgiveness programs. Because programs like Colorado's require teachers to obtain loans to pay for their coursework up front, however, teachers may prefer grants or scholarships that pay directly for classes as teachers take them.

Reimbursing teachers for education and training is another form of financial assistance that increases teachers' access to professional devel-opment. Usually, states restrict reimbursements to approved courses and trainings—often those that may be applied to earning college credits and/or a credential. Such restrictions help to ensure that ECE teachers do not pursue random professional development experiences, but those that are coordinated and/or linked systematically with credentials or degrees. In Hawaii, for instance, ECE teachers are eligible to be reimbursed for col-lege courses specific to early childhood, community-based workshops that may be converted to college credits, or assessment fees for obtaining a CDA certificate (PATCH, 2004). Maryland offers training reimbursement as an incentive to both center-based teachers and FCC providers to pursue the state's tiered child care credential. Participants receive reimbursement for each course, workshop, or conference—up to $400 combined in any given year (Maryland State Department of Education, 2005). Although these efforts appear modest and require an up-front investment of teachers' own resources, giving ECE teachers a financial means to pursue professional development acknowledges the crucial role that formal education and training play in producing high-quality teaching.

Articulation. Establishing and streamlining articulation between 2- and 4-year IHEs is a third approach to increasing teachers' access to professional development. Changing requirements, limited ease of access, and demanding schedules translate into ECE teachers taking a disjointed array of professional development courses and trainings at a variety of institutions and organizations. Often of little use to ECE teachers, this mixed bag of efforts does not yield them formal recognition, qualify them for enhanced compensation, or systematically improve their classroom practice. Therefore, to increase teachers' access to advanced degree programs and to help them translate their effort and experience into valuable degrees, mechanisms are sorely needed to allow teachers to utilize this mix of credits. These mechanisms, known as articulation agreements, link courses and credits together so that they can be applied toward formal degree requirements. They come in many forms: institution-to-institution articulation agreements, common course numbering, a general education common core, associate's degrees with guaranteed admission to a 4-year program, and transfer agreements (Shkodriani, 2004).

Examples of articulation mechanisms abound throughout the states. One popular mechanism for facilitating articulation is the Associate of Arts in Teaching (AAT) degree, which, unlike the traditional Associate in Applied Science (AAS) degree in Early Childhood Education, offers community college credit that parallels the first 2 years of a baccalaureate program in teacher education. Maryland developed the nation's first AAT to ensure a fully articulated transfer of credits from community colleges to any of the 22 four-year public and independent institutions offering teacher education programs in the state. Community colleges that offer the AAT must follow standards set by the Maryland Higher Education Commission (Shkodriani, 2004).

Connecticut's comprehensive articulation efforts ensure that ECE teachers have opportunities to translate prior learning into more advanced levels of professional development. To convert on-the-job experience and training into college credits, ECE teachers can take the Early Childhood Pathways exam sponsored by Connecticut Charts-A-Course (CCAC). This exam evaluates teachers' knowledge in two subjects: early childhood education and child developmental psychology. Teachers who pass the exam receive three college credits for each subject (Connecticut Charts-A-Course, 2005). All community colleges in Connecticut that offer early childhood associate's degree programs accept these credits, and, since Connecticut's 4-year IHEs have articulation agreements with its community colleges, success on the Pathways exam ultimately can count toward a BA.

Enhancing Professional Development Content

While increasing access to professional development opportunities is critical, ensuring that those opportunities are of high quality is equally important. Policies and programs that target the quality of professional development take three primary forms. First, policymakers and professional organizations are examining carefully the content and quality of formal education programs (i.e., 2- and 4-year colleges) and specialized training that prepare ECE teachers. A second type of effort strives to align the content of professional development with state-developed early learning standards (i.e., documents that specify what children should know and be able to do); these standards, in and of themselves, represent an effort to improve quality and increase accountability in ECE. Third, there are emerging efforts to align the content of professional development across different program types. Often defined in "core knowledge" documents, these efforts recognize that teachers, regardless of the setting in which they work, share the need for a similar body of knowledge in order to be well prepared.

Examining the Content of Formal Education and Specialized Training. National professional organizations currently are examining the content and quality of ECE teacher preparation programs at 2- and 4-year colleges and universities. As discussed in Chapter 5, variations in ECE teacher preparation programs across the country raise concerns about the consistency of quality instruction in higher education programs and, in turn, its influence on the quality of ECE teachers and child outcomes. For example, ECE teachers graduating from some programs may experience an emphasis on content knowledge and theory, whereas graduates from other programs may experience more practice in actual ECE settings—educational approaches with potentially different results for pedagogy. To ensure that IHEs provide high-quality education that incorporates elements of content knowledge, theory, and practice, the National Association for the Education of Young Children (NAEYC) and the National Council for the

Accreditation of Teacher Education (NCATE) developed five standards for ECE teacher preparation programs:

Standard 1. Promoting Child Development and Learning
Standard 2. Building Family and Community Relationships
Standard 3. Observing, Documenting, and Assessing to Support Young Children and Families
Standard 4. Teaching and Learning
Standard 5. Becoming a Professional (NAEYC, 2001, p. 11)

Two- and 4-year colleges and universities that implement these standards for their early childhood programs help ensure that students receive comprehensive content-area coursework and field experiences. Currently, 185 NCATE-accredited IHEs across the country offer NAEYC-approved advanced degrees, and five additional 2-year institutions, which are not eligible for NCATE accreditation, earned NAEYC accreditation in Spring 2006 (National Association for the Education of Young Children, 2006a; National Council for Accreditation of Teacher Education, 2007).

Turning from improving the content of formal education to improving the content of training, several efforts are underway. For example, to improve the quality of specialized training, the National Association of Child Care Resource and Referral Agencies (NACCRRA) currently is developing quality standards for training provided by child care resource and referral agencies (CCR&Rs) throughout the country. These standards will establish a trainer credential, educate trainers to use approved techniques that reflect and incorporate how teachers learn, and analyze the content of training. In addition to these efforts, NACCRRA is establishing criteria to ensure that CCR&Rs across the country offer high-quality specialized training and follow best practices for technical assistance. NACCRRA will recognize CCR&Rs that meet the criteria through an accreditation process (L. Smith, personal communication, July 2006).

Alignment of Professional Development with Early Learning Standards. Another effort to improve the content of ECE professional development focuses on the alignment of early learning standards with professional development efforts. Early learning standards, describing what children should know and be able to do, are proliferating across the United States. As of 2004, 41 states had developed early learning standards (Scott-Little, Kagan, & Frelow, 2005). This movement has been spurred, in part, by Good Start Grow Smart (GSGS), President George W. Bush's early childhood initiative, which requires states to develop voluntary early learning standards in language and literacy as a prerequisite for receiving Child Care Development Fund monies. In many cases, states are creating far more comprehensive standards and are including areas of cognitive, physical, motor, social, and emotional development. What is notable about GSGS is that it now is calling upon states to examine their professional development offerings vis-à-vis their early learning standards. If states are setting guidelines for children's development and learning, they also should be striving to prepare teachers to nurture and teach children in ways that are most relevant to and supportive of those standards.

To this end, several states have initiated efforts to align professional development efforts with their early learning standards. In Wisconsin, for example, completion of the state's early learning standards led to a review of the early childhood curriculum within the technical college system. As a result of this review, 2- and 4-year colleges and universities are unifying courses throughout the state and facilitating articulation agreements between institutions (Mitchell & LeMoine, 2005). Another effort to align coursework with early learning standards is taking place in Ohio, where IHEs throughout the state have created a staff position of Early Learning Specialist to facilitate the infusion of early learning standards into higher education coursework. Other states are aligning professional development with early learning standards by modifying their ECE teacher credentials to include training that specifically addresses the early learning standards. Maryland, for example, has embedded in its child care credential the expectation that teachers will receive training in the content and use of the state's early learning standards (Child Care Bureau, 2004b).

Alignment of Professional Development Content across Program Types. As noted earlier, states and ECE programs have very different entry and ongoing requirements for ECE teachers. In most states, an organization (a "registry") exists whose mission is to catalog ECE teachers' training and formal education attainment. The National Registry Alliance is an organization, comprising a number of state-level registries, that charts and coordinates professional development across ECE and school-age program types and across states. Recently, the National Registry Alliance partnered with NACCRRA to develop common definitions and classifications for specialized formal education and training that apply across different program types and across states (Martinez-Beck & Zaslow, 2006). Because many ECE teachers access specialized training, these efforts will have a unifying effect on expectations for ECE teacher knowledge, professional development opportunities, and workforce data collection, thereby equalizing the professional development of the ECE workforce writ large.

As suggested above, some states are already making progress in aligning professional development content across program types. West Virginia, for example, has defined core knowledge that all teachers should have irrespective of the program or program type in which they work. Aligned with the state's early learning standards, West Virginia's core knowledge expectations provide the foundation for the state's training and registry system, ensuring that training is available to ECE teachers in all aspects of core knowledge and in each domain of the state's early learning standards. In addition, West Virginia's core knowledge is guiding the development of training and education, such as a new college-level summer institute for prekindergarten teachers (Child Care Bureau, 2004b). By aligning expectations for teachers across all ECE program types, West Virginia is ensuring that teachers—those in Head Start, prekindergarten, child care, and family child care—have access to consistent professional development opportunities, and that all children enrolled in ECE have access to high-quality programs.

Supporting Specialized Professional Development

In addition to the professional development improvement efforts already discussed, there is an important group of efforts targeted to specific content (i.e., literacy) and/or to specific populations (i.e., infants and toddlers, children who are from diverse backgrounds and may speak more than one language, and children with disabilities). We discuss these as the fourth type of targeted efforts to improve ECE teachers' professional development.

Literacy. One key effort at the national level is the U.S. Department of Education's Early Childhood Educator Professional Development grant program, provided for in Title II of No Child Left Behind. This initiative aims to expand ECE teachers' access to professional development that enhances the quality of literacy instruction provided to young children living in low-income communities. It offers competitive grants for the creation of training and education for ECE teachers to support early literacy and language development. Local grantees, including institutions of higher education and other bodies that provide ECE professional development, may use these resources to develop training for teachers that addresses current and growing needs in the field, especially for teachers who work with English language learners and children with disabilities (U.S. Department of Education, 2004; Welch-Ross et al., 2006).

Infants and Toddlers. During the first 3 years of life, children undergo such dramatic developmental changes that ECE teachers working with this population need education and training specifically tailored to infants and toddlers. Sponsored by the federal Child Care Bureau, the National Infant and Toddler Child Care Initiative at Zero to Three supports infant and toddler care on a national level. Through this initiative, states learn from one another about best policies and practices to promote and improve infant/toddler care. The initiative supports states in the development of specific policies that improve the quality of infant and toddler child care, including quality rating systems, credentials targeted specifically to infant/toddler care, and networks that provide technical assistance focused on infant/toddler development and care (National Infant & Toddler Child Care Initiative, 2004).

To further support ECE for infants and toddlers, a portion of the Child Care Development Fund allocation focuses on infant/toddler program quality improvement. In FY 2006, this earmark reached more than $98 million nationally (Child Care Bureau, 2006). States are using this funding to advance professional development, including training programs focused specifically on instructing ECE teachers to implement curricula tailored to the needs of very young children. Eighteen states, for example, are using WestEd's Program for Infant/Toddler Caregivers (PITC), designed to improve center-based teachers' and FCC providers' instruction and care of infants and toddlers (Johnson-Staub, 2005; National Infant & Toddler Child Care Initiative, 2004). PITC includes a train-the-trainer program and on-site training for ECE teachers. Through a series of pre- and posttraining studies without randomized control groups, WestEd's Center for Child and Family Studies has found positive relationships between PITC training/technical assistance and teacher quality. In these studies, teacher quality was assessed before and after teachers participated in PITC training/technical assistance services that ranged in duration from 6 to 9 months (WestEd Center for Child and Family Studies, 2003, 2006). Encouraged by these results, WestEd is currently working with an independent evaluator that is conducting a randomized study of the PITC's effects on teacher quality and child outcomes. It is anticipated that the first set of results from this study will be available in the fall of 2008 (P. Mangione & K. Kriener-Althen, personal communication, May 10, 2007).

Other states—Utah and Wisconsin, for example—are establishing sets of training requirements that lead to an endorsement or credential specifically acknowledging teachers' qualifications to work with infants and toddlers. Utah's Infant/Toddler Endorsement requires 40 hours of specialized training that is provided through the CCR&R system. Caregivers interested in earning Wisconsin's Infant/Toddler Credential complete 12 credits of coursework, including a Capstone Experience (National Infant & Toddler Child Care Initiative, 2006).

Linguistic and Cultural Diversity. The United States is becoming increasingly linguistically and culturally diverse: From 1990 to 2000 the percentage of Americans who identified themselves as Hispanic, Black, American Indian, Asian, and other grew by 43%, and non-Hispanic Whites accounted for 7% less of the population. Because of these trends and because at least one study has found that ECE teachers who communicate effectively with children and their parents are more effective (Garcia, Jensen, & Cuellar, 2006), there is an urgent need to develop a workforce equipped to interact with young children in linguistically and culturally appropriate ways (Garcia, 2001).

In 1999, the National Center for Education Statistics (NCES) reported that more than half of all ECE teachers taught students who had limited English proficiency or were from cultural backgrounds different from their own (in Early & Winton, 2001). Therefore, increasing the number of new ECE teachers from racial and ethnic minorities, as well as those who speak languages other than English, is crucial. One strategy for enhancing ECE teachers' linguistic and cultural competence is through education and training programs that emphasize these skills. Indeed, encouraging all ECE teachers, regardless of race or language spoken, to participate in formal diversity education or training may be an effective and more immediate means of enhancing cultural sensitivity within the ECE teaching workforce. In Illinois, for example, the Birth to Five Project, facilitated by the Ounce of Prevention Fund, convened a Bilingual/Bicultural Ad Hoc Workgroup to recommend systemic solutions "to the issues and challenges of working successfully with children and families who are English language learners or who identify with cultures different from the predominant U.S. culture" (Ounce of Prevention Fund, 2005). The workgroup focuses on recruiting and retaining a highly qualified bilingual/bicultural ECE workforce by targeting certification processes to the achievement of bilingualism and biculturalism, and by organizing workshops for ongoing professional development (J. Weiner, personal communication, March 2, 2006).

Unfortunately, across the country, formal education requirements to prepare teachers to work effectively with culturally and linguistically diverse populations are limited. An analysis of course requirements for 167 higher education programs for ECE teachers found that most universities required students to take only one semester hour or less of "diversity" coursework, 3% of universities required students to have a teaching placement in a "diverse" setting, and 20% required future teachers to take foreign language courses (Ray et al., 2006). Although far too limited, there are important efforts targeted to increasing diversity training provided to the ECE workforce. Head Start, specifically, has taken strides to enhance professional development opportunities that support its teaching workforce's ability to understand, respect, and work with diversity. For example, through a Head Start grant to support a Head Start–Higher Education

Hispanic Latino Service Partnership, the University of Texas–San Antonio has implemented a Summer Institute to meet the educational needs of teachers, counselors, social workers, and directors from Head Start programs that serve predominantly Hispanic clients (Office of Head Start, 2004).

Children with Disabilities. While every high-quality ECE teacher should differentiate instruction and make accommodations to meet every child's unique needs, teachers working with children with disabilities face particular challenges in this regard. Teachers of children with disabilities must understand how disabilities affect children's interactions, relationships, growth, and learning. They must understand how to meet the special needs and particular challenges of children with cognitive and other developmental delays. They also must collaborate with parents and early intervention specialists who are integral to the educative process. The research suggests, though, that education and training that accomplish all of this are limited. In a survey of ECE teachers, of the 71% who taught students with special needs, only 17% felt well prepared to meet the needs of these children (NCES in Early & Winton, 2001). These data show there is a need to expand and enhance professional development that focuses on teaching children with disabilities.

ECE teacher certification is one mechanism for increasing the likelihood that all teachers working with children with disabilities are prepared to do so. New research on the benefits of inclusive education, which integrates all children, has led many states to adopt joint early childhood education–early childhood special education certificates (M. Bruder, personal communication, July 2006). Similarly, a recent trend in many teacher preparation programs is to require all teachers to take coursework in both general and special education (Stayton & McCollum, 2002). Despite these shifts, national research shows that bachelor's degree programs in early childhood education require teachers to take an average of just 8.62 semester hours of coursework that addresses primarily or only special education (Ray et al., 2006).

Efforts at the national and state levels are increasing awareness of the need for, and opportunities for teachers to participate in, specialized professional development focused on working with children with disabilities. Nationally, the U.S. Department of Education's Office of Special Education Programs (OSEP) has an Early Childhood Team that administers discretionary grants, cooperative agreements, and contracts for projects that directly support improving services for infants, toddlers, and preschoolers with disabilities (U.S. Department of Education, n.d.). In FY 2004, for example, OSEP funded 117 personnel preparation projects and currently supports the National Early Childhood Technical Assistance Center (NECTAC), which focuses specifically on supporting special education teachers for children birth to age 5. NECTAC serves as a clearinghouse for policy and research on children with disabilities; it also offers technical assistance to states to ensure that children with disabilities and their families receive high-quality services (National Early Childhood Technical Assistance Center, n.d.).

In addition to OSEP, the federal Child Care Bureau and the Head Start Bureau jointly support the Center on the Social and Emotional Foundations for Early Learning (CSEFEL), an initiative that enhances ECE for children with disabilities (Center on the Social and Emotional Foundations for Early Learning, n.d.). CSEFEL develops and disseminates evidence-based information and works with existing training and technical assistance providers to help ECE teachers meet the needs of children with challenging behaviors and with mental health challenges. In addition, in Head Start and Early Head Start programs, where more than 10% of enrolled children have special needs, teachers receive specialized training to work in inclusive settings. For instance, the Hilton/Early Head Start Training Program is a public/private partnership between the Conrad N. Hilton Foundation and the Head Start Bureau that helps Early Head Start and Migrant and Seasonal Head Start staff and family members learn strategies to support children with significant disabilities. The program's signature effort, SpecialQuest, provides training and learning coaches to teams of administrators, early interventionists, teachers, and parents to help them better serve children with disabilities (California Institute on Human Services and Sonoma State University, n.d.).

Innovations at the state level also are enhancing teachers' skills in working with children with disabilities. For instance, North Carolina's Partnerships for Inclusion (PFI) is a statewide technical assistance project that offers training, on-site consultation, product development, and conferences to support teachers working in inclusive settings with children with disabilities. PFI's offerings are based on the premise that intensive, meaningful, and ongoing professional development is far more effective than one-time workshops in increasing adults' learning about teaching children with disabilities. PFI's innovative consultation model includes one-on-one guidance provided to teachers across multiple visits over a period of 5 to 8 months. Teachers have incentives to participate in PFI's training —not only because it helps improve their classroom practice, but also because it fulfills North Carolina's ongoing training requirements (Palsha & Wesley, 1998; Wesley, 1994).

Individualizing Professional Development

The fifth and final targeted approach to improving professional development takes the form of individualized support to teachers by skilled colleagues within the context of the ECE classroom. Mentoring, coaching, peer review and assistance, and home-based technical assistance programs provide individualized, on-site support to ECE teachers. These individualized professional development efforts often are subsumed under the general term "mentoring." To lend more precision to our discussion and illustrate different program models, we distinguish mentoring programs from other individualized professional development programs.

Mentoring Programs. Mentoring programs support student teachers or newly employed teachers by providing them with individualized training and feedback from qualified supervisors or colleagues. Mentoring programs orient prospective and new teachers (protégés) to ECE with the goal of improving their teaching and sustaining their longevity in the program and field. Mentoring serves to induct new workers into ECE using many informal and individualized strategies. At least 21 states have mentoring programs (National Child Care Information Center, 2006b; Twombly, Montilla, & De Vita, 2001).

The California Early Childhood Mentor Program (CECMP), for example, established in 1988, is the country's largest mentoring program for ECE teachers, providing mentors for new ECE teachers and less experienced administrators. CECMP selects mentors based on their work in high-quality programs and their ability to provide excellent guidance to high school, community college, and university student-teachers embarking on careers in ECE (California Early Childhood Mentor Program, n.d.). Participating mentors receive recognition and additional compensation for their services. Results from an evaluation of CECMP showed that ECE programs that incorporated mentors had lower staff turnover than the average rate of turnover in the field (California Early Childhood Mentor Program, n.d.).

In several states, including Minnesota, South Dakota, Washington State, and Tennessee, mentoring programs target FCC providers (Minnesota Licensed Family Child Care Association, 2006; South Dakota Department of Social Services, 2006; Tennessee Family Child Care Alliance, 2006; Washington State Child Care Resource and Referral Network, 2006). Because home-based FCC providers often feel isolated, mentors may provide information and resources on child development and program administration to providers, building meaningful relationships to help integrate them into the greater ECE field.

Apprenticeship programs, more structured forms of mentoring programs, provide a highly structured combination of formal education and on-the-job guidance, with the goal of attracting and retaining new ECE teachers. In 1999, the U.S. Department of Labor (DOL) initiated a formal apprenticeship program to recruit and train ECE teachers in both center- and home-based settings under the direction of qualified individuals. From 2000 to 2003, the DOL awarded grants to establish the apprenticeship program in 31 states and the District of Columbia. The program, which requires apprentices to complete at least 4,000 hours of on-the-job training over approximately 2 years in addition to a minimum of 144 hours of related higher education coursework per year, awards practitioners with college credit and increased compensation as they progress through the apprenticeship. State grantees reported that the apprenticeship program increased the availability of training, improved the quality of child care, and helped to stabilize the teaching workforce by decreasing turnover. In addition, as a result of attaining higher levels of education and greater feelings of professionalism, FCC providers increased the fees they charged families, thereby increasing their compensation. With encouragement from the DOL, at least 16 of the 31 states extended the apprenticeship program with state funding (U.S. Department of Labor Employment and Training Administration, 2005).

Curriculum Consultants and/or Coaches. Curriculum consultants and coaches provide individualized support for teachers by introducing them to new teaching methods and guiding their application of new methods in the classroom. Whereas mentoring and apprenticeship programs focus primarily on recruiting new teachers, consultation and coaching efforts work to improve the practices of experienced teachers. Research suggests that coaches and consultants play many distinct roles in supporting ECE teachers. They may serve as strategists, translators, advocates, nurturers, teachers, learners, professional role models, and curriculum developers (Rust & Freidus in Ryan, Hornbeck, & Frede, 2004).

Currently, the Frank Porter Graham Child Development Institute is conducting the Quality Interventions for Early Care and Education (QUINCE) study of two assessment-based, individualized on-site consultation models: (1) the Partnerships for Inclusion program, in which teachers work toward personal quality improvement goals over several months, and (2) the Rameys' Immersion Training for Excellence consultation model, which provides a compressed consultation program with approximately 20 sequential full days of on-site consultation. While both consultation models support teachers in center-based and home-based settings, the QUINCE study has a particular focus on the impact of the intervention on the quality and effectiveness of FCC providers and FFN caregivers (Frank Porter Graham Child Development Institute, 2006). Given the prevalence of home-based ECE and the dearth of evaluations on related professional development initiatives, these evaluations will help to fill a severe data gap in the field.

Peer Assistance and Review Programs. Peer assistance and review is one model of individualized on-the-job support that has not yet been widely implemented in ECE, although it is more established in the K–12 education system. The premise of peer assistance and review programs is to pair high-quality teachers with new teachers or teachers who are having difficulty in the classroom (Laurence et al., 2002). In these efforts, teachers develop collaborative relationships, with the goals of supporting one another and improving instruction. In K–12 settings where this is operative, the peer relationship is evaluative, with the experienced teacher assessing the quality of her peer's teaching. Unlike other forms of individualized professional development, though, peer assistance and review may lead to the termination of teachers who fail to meet performance standards for classroom teaching.

The Toledo Federation of Teachers created the first peer assistance and review model, called the Toledo Plan, for K–12 teachers (Toledo Public Schools and Toledo Federation of Teachers, 2002). In Toledo, new and/or struggling teachers are paired with consulting teachers who must have a minimum of 5 years of outstanding teaching service and who receive additional compensation for their work. Until the new or struggling teachers successfully meet established performance standards, a decision made with the help of the consulting teacher, they are designated as probationary employees of the school district and probationary union members. In Toledo, this standard resulted in 8% of nontenured teachers and 90 tenured teachers being terminated from employment with the school district (Moses, 2006). Since the advent of the Toledo Plan, other school districts have adopted peer assistance and review professional development models. Currently, between 75 and 80 programs implement some form of the Toledo Plan (Moses, 2006). In Rochester, New York, for example, the peer assistance program was credited with raising the retention of beginning teachers from 60% to 90% (Recruiting New Teachers in Laurence et al., 2002).

Home-Based Technical Assistance for FCC Providers and FFN Caregivers. Visiting programs for ECE teachers in home-based programs, also known as home-based technical assistance, are yet another form of individualized mentoring or coaching that targets improved professional development. Because the vast majority of FCC and FFN teachers are not in settings with other early childhood staff, some visiting program efforts aim to connect independent providers and caregivers to others in the field. Several states have established home visiting programs to enhance the quality of education and care provided to children in home-based settings.

FCC providers may seek to take advantage of the professional development opportunities available to ECE teachers, but they often face barriers in accessing these opportunities. Barriers include the lack of knowledge that the opportunities exist, as well as the lack of "release time," substitute teachers, and financial resources necessary for full engagement in high-quality professional development. As a result, some states and localities have developed home visiting programs to improve FCC providers' practices (Hamm et al., 2005). In these programs, a consultant goes to the provider's home and offers one-on-one training, perhaps engaging in model teaching. For example, the Good Beginnings Never End project in Long Beach, California, conducts home visits tailored to support each provider's circumstances, using the learning areas in the Family Day Care Rating Scale as guidance. This project also plans field trips to connect providers with community resources, such as local libraries, and with one another (Hamm et al., 2005). Beyond training, home visitors serve as a source of information and moral support for providers.

Home-based technical assistance for FFN caregivers can have both monitoring and professional development functions. According to Porter and Kearns (2005), six states, Georgia, Idaho, New Jersey, Louisiana, Arizona, and Arkansas, mandate home inspections for FFN caregivers who receive child care subsidies. In addition, four states—Alaska, Louisiana, Missouri, and New Jersey—offer home visiting to FFN caregivers. Missouri's Project REACH (Rural Early Childhood Educational Institute) offers FFN caregivers monthly visits during which consultants assess caregivers' practice and then, together, consultants and caregivers work to improve different aspects of care via modeling and other strategies (Center for Family Policy and Research, 2005; Porter & Kearns, 2005).

EFFORTS TO INCREASE COMPENSATION

Within the top tier of the pyramid, the second type of targeted effort to support and enhance the ECE workforce encompasses initiatives that increase ECE teachers' compensation. Some of these initiatives emphasize hourly wage or annual salary enhancements, while others emphasize benefit enhancements that include pensions, health care, paid sick or vacation days, and other nonsalary compensation. Both wages and benefits, the two elements of compensation, are sorely in need of enhancement.

As discussed in Chapters 3 and 5, compensation for ECE teachers is extraordinarily low, unreflective of professional qualifications, and widely discrepant across program type. Additionally, as increased compensation has been shown to correlate with both stability among ECE teachers (Whitebook et al., 1998; Whitebook & Sakai, 2003; Whitebook et al., 2001) and increased educational quality (Barnett, 2003b; Phillips et al., 2001), wage and benefit initiatives may be especially effective tools in the effort to improve ECE experiences for young children.

Wage Initiatives

Wage enhancement efforts effectively set a minimum or living wage above federal and state minimum wage levels for a segment of the population. In some cases, the efforts are targeted specifically to ECE teachers; in other cases, the efforts apply to a broad population of human services employees, with ECE teachers being one eligible population. Because of the federal political system in the United States, in which states and localities often set their own minimum wage standards above and beyond that established by the federal government, living wage policies generally are launched at the local level and require local governments' support for both enforcement and funding. Across the country, there are approximately 140 local living wage laws, many of which specifically target ECE teachers' low salaries.

San Francisco, for example, implemented a living wage initiative in 1999 to complement other ECE workforce policies (City and County of San Francisco Department of Human Services, 2004). Called WAGES *Plus* (Wage Augmentation Entry-Level Staff Plus), the initiative supplements the hourly wage of ECE teachers and support staff. The amount of the hourly supplement is derived from the difference between a teacher's hourly pay and an applicable wage floor. Wage floors are based on a combination of teachers' education and work responsibilities. In 2001, San Francisco expanded the basic WAGES *Plus* program to reward teachers' longevity in the field and their professional qualifications, as well as to include FCC providers. An evaluation of the WAGES *Plus* program found that, compared with nonparticipants, participants were better compensated, intended to stay in the field longer, were more likely to pursue professional development, were more likely to have taken unit-bearing ECE courses, and had greater feelings of professionalism (LaFrance et al., 2004).

Other localities subsume living wage policies for ECE teachers under broader wage initiatives. For example, in 2000, the Denver City Council adopted a living wage requirement for employees of any city contractor or subcontractor who held a position as parking lot attendant, security guard, clerical support worker, or child care worker on city-owned or city-leased property (Living Wage Resource Center, 2005). Although the scope of this wage enhancement effort is broad, only those ECE teachers who have contracts with the City and County of Denver benefit.

In countries with more centralized government and governance systems, it is possible to implement wage enhancement policies that affect the entire ECE teaching workforce. In Great Britain and Australia, for instance, all ECE teachers earn a minimum wage that has been established by a national review board (Helburn & Bergmann, 2002; UNESCO, 2006). In Australia, minimum wage levels are determined according to teachers' qualifications and experience. ECE programs are monitored to ensure that they comply with the minimum wage policy. Although promising because of their comprehensive application to all ECE teachers, it is important to note that these efforts do not link the minimum wage policy with other policies that ensure that higher wages actually yield higher quality ECE. Evaluations of minimum wage efforts indicate that ECE programs (especially for-profit ones) often respond by cutting program costs instead of raising additional revenue; in order to compete for clients (families and their children), programs must keep their costs down and offer the lowest cost care possible. Cost-cutting measures such as exceeding appropriate child to staff ratios compromise the quality of care available to all families (Wannan, 2005).

Benefit Initiatives

Because the ECE industry is composed of a multitude of small businesses operating under different auspices, the cost of benefits is very expensive for individual private or community-based ECE programs. Benefits, especially health care coverage, depend on having a critical number of employees to share the costs of those benefits, and so ECE teachers in very large programs (e.g., Military Child Care) or within certain program types (e.g., public schools) may have access to health insurance while their counterparts in community-based child care programs may not. Each initiative discussed below draws ECE teachers into a larger personnel pool, creating an economy of scale that makes the provision of benefits affordable and feasible.

The state of Rhode Island has implemented benefit initiatives that assist both center-based and home-based ECE teachers in acquiring health insurance. Child care centers may receive state assistance to provide their employees with health insurance through the Starting RIght Health Care Insurance Assistance Program. The state contributes $85 per month per employee to licensed child care centers that offer employer-sponsored health insurance. To be an eligible center, 40% of the enrolled children must receive child care subsidies and the center must match the state's financial contribution before passing any health insurance costs on to employees. The Rhode Island Department of Human Services's Child Care Provider RIte Care (CCPRC) offers health insurance to FCC providers who are not covered by the state's health insurance program for low-income families. As of 2005, the regulations stipulated that FCC providers must have received at least $7,800 in reimbursements for serving children who receive child care subsidies in the 6 months prior to submitting an application for health insurance assistance (Rhode Island Department of Human Services, 2005). However, this policy changed during the 2005 legislative session to require all FCC providers to apply for the health insurance coverage through the state's child health insurance program before applying for the CCPRC health insurance program. The legislative change also limited enrollment to providers whose family income was less than 350% of the federal poverty level ($67,725 for a family of four). As a result, enrollment in CCPRC has dropped since 2005.

In North Carolina, the T.E.A.C.H. (Teacher Education and Compensation Helps) Early Childhood® Health Insurance Program helps fund the cost of health insurance for individuals working in child care programs that have made a commitment to support the education and compensation of their staff. ECE teachers must work in eligible programs in which (1) staff members participate in the T.E.A.C.H. Early Childhood® Project, or (2) all teaching and administrative staff have 2- or 4-year degrees in child development or early childhood education. Any licensed FCC provider who has a 2- or 4-year degree in these fields or who has a T.E.A.C.H. Early Childhood® scholarship also may participate. Participants purchase health insurance in the market and are then reimbursed up to one-third of the cost, paid from a special fund administered by North Carolina's Division of Child Development (Child Care Services Association, 2004).

EFFORTS TO IMPROVE WORK ENVIRONMENTS

Also in the top tier of the pyramid, work environment strategies constitute the third major type of targeted effort to improve the ECE teaching workforce. In contrast to professional development efforts and compensation strategies—both directly focused on ECE teachers as employees—work environment strategies are designed to improve the overall working conditions experienced by teachers in their programs. As such, they may have an indirect, but nonetheless crucial, impact on teachers themselves.

Paula Jorde-Bloom has conducted considerable research on productive work environments for ECE teachers. In her analysis of center-based programs' organizational climate, Jorde-Bloom (1988) identified 10 dimensions of organizational climate that contribute to teachers' job satisfaction: (1) collegiality, (2) professional growth, (3) supervisor support, (4) clarity (of policies and procedures), (5) reward system, (6) decision making, (7) goal consensus, (8) task orientation, (9) physical setting, and (10) innovativeness. These 10 dimensions can be encouraged, implemented, and sustained either by improving the skills of the people in leadership positions within programs or by improving the managerial and administrative processes and practices used in ECE work environments. We first discuss efforts that improve the skills of people, notably program administrators, and then turn to a discussion of efforts to improve administrative and managerial processes and practices.

Improving the Skills of Program Administrators

Administrators play a critical role in creating supportive work environments through effective supervision and strong leadership (Jorde-Bloom & Sheerer, 1992; Hayden in Muijs et al., 2004). As indicated in Chapter 4, some evidence suggests effective supervisors can create environments in which teachers are more responsive to children and more likely to engage children in language play and other developmentally appropriate practices (Howes et al., 2003). Administrators who provide coaching, support, constructive feedback, and recognition for good performance help their employees provide high-quality ECE (Crandall, 2004; Jorde-Bloom, 1988; Whitebook & Bellm, 1999). Moreover, when directors are supportive, teachers who participate in high-quality, specialized training are more likely to implement newly learned practices (Blase, 1999).

By fostering directors' leadership qualities, management skills, and administrative knowledge through formal mechanisms like training and credentials, states promote supportive work environments for ECE teachers. Although training in program administration has been shown to improve the overall work environment (Jorde-Bloom & Sheerer, 1992), only 15 states have regulations requiring directors to participate in either entry or ongoing training in program administration (LeMoine & Azer, 2006b). To support improvement of administrators' and directors' effectiveness, some states have established credentials that specifically recognize leadership competence. Florida, Oklahoma, and North Carolina are the only states that require directors to have a credential (LeMoine & Azer, 2006c). For example, Oklahoma's child care licensing requirements mandate that all directors achieve one of three credential levels: bronze, silver, or gold. Oklahoma provides financial awards as an incentive for directors to pursue more advanced credentials.

Improving Administrative and Managerial Processes and Practices

A second strategy to improve the overall work environment is the use of management and administration assessment tools. These tools guide programs through self-analysis and improvement processes. Each tool discussed below is designed to complement assessment tools that consider overall program and classroom quality (e.g., NAEYC accreditation, the Early Childhood Environment Rating Scale [ECERS]) by assessing administrative practices.

The Center for the Child Care Workforce created the Model Work Standards to assess the administration and working conditions of center-based, home-based, and after-school child care programs. This resource outlines essential elements (e.g., salary scales for all positions) as well as ideal elements (e.g., annual cost-of-living increases for staff) that contribute to a successful work environment. Teachers and directors can use these standards to evaluate and improve their workplace. Similar assessment instruments for center-based programs' work environments have been developed by the McCormick Tribune Center for Early Childhood Leadership. The Early Childhood Work Environment Survey (ECWES), a measure of overall organizational climate, assesses ECE teachers' perceptions and attitudes about co-worker relations, supervisor support, decision-making influence, goal consensus, and physical setting. More recently, the Program Administration Scale (PAS) (Talan & Bloom, 2005) has been developed to measure the quality of ECE programs' administrative practices. This tool provides a comprehensive assessment of the overall administration of programs, examining 10 areas of administration: (1) human resources development, (2) personnel cost and allocation, (3) center operations, (4) child assessment, (5) fiscal management, (6) program planning and evaluation, (7) family partnerships, (8) marketing and public relations, (9) technology, and (10) staff qualifications (McCormick Tribune Center for Early Childhood Leadership, 2005).

Although the PAS is a relatively new assessment instrument, it has become popular with local municipalities, state agencies, and Head Start grantees that seek to improve ECE workplace environments (T. Talan, personal communication, April 2006). Currently, Chicago's Department of Children and Youth Services is assessing the quality of all 400 of its Head Start and child care programs, using the PAS to measure administrative practices and the ECERS to measure classroom practices. Building on this approach, Arkansas, Illinois, and Ohio have developed comprehensive plans to incorporate the PAS into their statewide quality rating systems ("Ohio, Arkansas, Illinois adopt NLU early childhood leadership quality rating tools," 2007).

CONCLUSION

It is clear that numerous efforts across the country are striving to target and improve ECE teachers' professional development, compensation, and work environments. Chapter 4 of this volume suggests that, to some degree, these targeted approaches may positively influence teacher quality and effectiveness. The data also show that existing policies and programs are varied and dispersed, with many initiatives limited to particular program types or subpopulations of the ECE teaching workforce. Such variation leads to considerable inequality of opportunity, experience, and rewards for ECE teachers: Being an ECE teacher in San Francisco, for instance, where there are both mentorship and compensation initiatives, provides more promising career opportunities than being an ECE teacher in many other localities. Similarly, teachers in state-funded prekindergarten programs have considerably different levels of professional qualifications and compensation than their counterparts in private child care programs. These inconsistencies in workforce opportunities perpetuate troublesome inequities in the programs and services offered to children both within states and across the nation.

While these inequities could be rectified by expanding programs proven successful by rigorous evaluation, the challenge of securing the political will and ongoing funding to take these initiatives to scale—either at the state level or nationally—is formidable. Of the efforts discussed in this chapter, increasing ECE teachers' compensation is perhaps the most challenging, not only because it will be costly to implement for all teachers in all settings, but also because increased compensation does not directly guarantee that ECE teachers will have higher qualifications or that children will experience higher quality ECE. Recognizing the crucial interconnections between teachers' qualifications, professional development, compensation, work environments, and child outcomes, many ECE workforce improvement efforts across the United States integrate multiple strategies in their missions. Some of these efforts, for example, focus on increasing compensation while concurrently raising the expected levels of professional development for ECE teachers. These integrated efforts are addressed in the next chapter.

Tier Two: Integrated Efforts

RETURNING TO the pyramid, the second tier encompasses those efforts that integrate multiple strategies in their quest to improve the ECE teaching workforce. Because ECE workforce challenges are interrelated, increasingly work-force improvement initiatives seek to address multiple challenges simultaneously. These policies and programs are classified as integrated efforts because they align multiple workforce policies and programs and are therefore broader than the targeted efforts discussed in Chapter 6. These policies and programs fall into four categories: (1) compensation and rewards linked with increased professional development, (2) efforts specific to program types, (3) unionization, and (4) collective management and shared services.

COMPENSATION AND REWARDS LINKED WITH INCREASED PROFESSIONAL DEVELOPMENT

The first major category of efforts in tier two of the pyramid includes initiatives that link teachers' compensation with their professional development. Integrated efforts linking compensation and professional development simultaneously achieve several goals: increasing ECE teachers' (a) participation in professional development activities and coursework, (b) attainment of formal education, and (c) hourly wages or annual salaries. The increases in compensation may occur either in the form of direct increases to teachers' base wage or salary or via stipends, awarded on an annual or semiannual basis. While one-time awards or salary supplements do increase teachers' income, they do not establish a permanent increase in teachers' base hourly wages or annual salaries; therefore, they do not constitute ongoing incentives for teachers to remain in the ECE field. The challenge, of course, is that such increases in base-level compensation require stable and predictable funding, something that, as noted in Chapter 5, is absent from the ECE market.

Existing data affirm that gains in teacher qualifications and compensation translate into greater feelings of professionalism and program benefits like lower levels of turnover and higher levels of program quality.

Research reveals additional unexpected benefits of efforts that link compensation with teachers' formal education and training: strengthened institutions of higher education, improved articulation among 2- and 4-year colleges and universities, development of career ladders, and creation of registries that catalog the training teachers receive (Child Care Services Association, 2005a; Whitebook & Bellm, 2004). There is, however, a dearth of research linking these efforts directly to improved teacher quality and effectiveness.

Within this category of integrated efforts that link compensation with increased professional development are state-based efforts to provide increased compensation to teachers who demonstrate they have attained higher levels of training and formal education. North Carolina pioneered one such effort with the Child Care WAGE$® Project, which provides semiannual salary supplements to teachers based on their level of education and training. Rewards range from $200 to $4,000, with greater amounts for teachers who have attained higher levels of education and training. Participants must be employed in a licensed child care center or FCC home and must remain in one workplace for at least 6 months. Teachers must work at least 10 hours per week serving children up to 5 years old and cannot earn more than $14.45 per hour to be eligible. In 2004–2005, evaluations of the Child Care WAGE$® Project showed that 60% of participants were taking classes and 97% of participants reported that the wage supplements influenced their pursuit of additional education. Participants also reported increased feelings of professionalism; 98% of responding directors indicated that they felt more appreciated and recognized, and 82% noted increases in staff morale and more positive interactions between children and teachers as a result of participating in the WAGE$® Project (Child Care Services Association, 2005a). Currently, the Child Care WAGE$® Project also is licensed to operate in Florida, Kansas, and South Carolina.

Other efforts have linked compensation increases to teachers' attainment of specific levels of training or formal education that promote a teacher along a career path, a formal codified progression of qualifications. For example, launched in 2000, the Washington State Child Care Career and Wage Ladder Pilot Project provided higher compensation to ECE teachers who moved up the career ladder by acquiring higher levels of education and more experience. The state shared the costs of increasing compensation with participating centers by paying not only 50% of the wage increases that resulted from adopting the Career and Wage Ladder, but also an additional 15% for administrative costs. To be eligible to participate, programs had to meet minimum quality criteria by (1) enrolling at least 10% subsidized children, (2) providing staff with a minimum of 10 days' annual paid leave, (3) providing staff with access to a health insurance plan, and (4) establishing a Quality Care Committee to address the over-all quality of the center. If more than 25% of the children enrolled in a participating center received child care subsidies, the state also rewarded teachers' experience with an additional wage increase. An evaluation of the pilot project found that it increased staff compensation, specialized training (although differences in hiring practices or applicant quality could explain this finding), professionalism, and program quality (Boyd & Wand-schneider, 2004). Although the pilot project was discontinued in 2003 because of budget cuts, the Washington State legislature established the Early Childhood Education Career and Wage Ladder in statute in 2005; in the following year, state general funds were appropriated to support it, although they fall short of the amount needed to fully implement the Ladder (Center for the Child Care Workforce, 2006b).

Recognizing that attaining higher levels of training and formal edu-cation may not be possible without providing teachers with additional supports, yet another kind of integrated initiative provides both incentives and compensation rewards for teachers' participation in professional de-velopment and attainment of higher qualifications. The Teacher Educa-tion and Compensation Helps (T.E.A.C.H.) Early Childhood® Project is the most widespread effort to enhance both the formal education and com-pensation of ECE teachers in center-based programs and licensed FCC homes. The model requires support from the state (usually in the form of program administration and funding), the ECE employer (usually in the form of workplace flexibility and funding), and the ECE teacher (in the form of dedication to the program of study and to the ECE workplace). Developed in 1990 by North Carolina's Child Care Services Association (CCSA), 22 states have adopted the T.E.A.C.H. Early Childhood® model (Child Care Services Association, 2005d; Russell & Rogers, 2005). There are four components of the program.

1. *Scholarships* that cover partial costs for tuition and books or assess-ment fees. Often, while states or private foundations pay for the scholarships, the ECE employer is required to provide the scholar-ship recipient with paid release time and a travel stipend.
2. *Education,* usually in the form of college coursework, to be com-pleted during a prescribed contract period by each participant in return for receiving a scholarship.
3. *Compensation,* paid by the employer to the participant after she has completed the education requirements and fulfilled the contract. Participants are eligible to receive increased compensation in the form of a one-time bonus (ranging from $100 to $700) or an on-going pay raise (4% or 5%), usually paid by the ECE employer.

4. *Commitment* from participants to stay in their current ECE setting or the field for 6 months to a year, depending on the scholarship program (Child Care Services Association, 2005c).

As a result of this initiative, more than 80,000 early childhood teachers, directors, and family child care providers nationally have been given the opportunity to access educational experiences and have been rewarded for doing so (Russell & Rogers, 2005). Evaluations of the T.E.A.C.H. Early Childhood® Project implemented in North Carolina found that the program met its goals of raising participating teachers' formal education, compensation, and retention (Child Care Services Association, 2005b). Evaluations of Wisconsin's T.E.A.C.H. Early Childhood® Project were similar: Project participants had much lower rates of turnover (12%) than the annual turnover rates for Wisconsin's ECE teachers in general (40%), and wage increases for recipients also exceeded average wage increases for ECE teachers across the state (Adams, Bierbrauer, Edie, Riley, & Roach, 2003). As suggested by Park-Jadotte, Golin, and Gault (2002), these results are not generalizable to the entire ECE workforce. Because participation in T.E.A.C.H. Early Childhood® is voluntary, participants are more likely to be motivated and committed to their work than the general ECE teaching population. In other words, if ECE teachers were *required* to participate, it is unclear whether the reductions in turnover noted above would be achieved. That said, these evaluations indicate that T.E.A.C.H. Early Childhood® can produce very positive results.

Yet another kind of initiative linking compensation with professional development rewards teachers who not only attain higher levels of training and education, but also continue to participate in professional development over time. An example exists in California, where counties throughout the state have implemented what is commonly referred to as CARES (Compensation and Recognition Encourages Stability) to reward ECE teachers' education and training with compensation supplements. Participating center-based staff (including teachers, site supervisors, and directors) and FCC providers must meet certain education and training qualifications, commit to continuing their professional development for at least 21 hours per year, and agree to provide ECE services for a specified period of time. Stipends are given to participating teachers annually and range from $500 to $6,000 per year, depending on participants' education and background (Whitebook & Bellm, 2004). Because there is no statewide, centralized administration of CARES, counties have adapted the model to address their needs. Thus there is some variation in the manner in which counties have implemented the initiative. This initiative reached nearly 50,000 ECE teachers in its first 4 years (First 5 California, 2006). Several evaluations of CARES have been conducted; one in San Mateo County showed that participants accumulated an average of 5.7 more units of formal education in ECE than nonparticipants (Whitebook & Bellm, 2004). Another evaluation conducted in Alameda County found that the program successfully increased the number of ECE teachers seeking training. Additional results from a qualitative study showed that the program increased demand for child development courses at local colleges and universities (Caspary, Gilman, & Hamilton, 2002).

Several states link compensation and professional development for FFN caregivers specifically. These efforts offer FFN caregivers stipends, reimbursement rate increases, or materials to encourage their participation in training. Alabama's Kids and Kin Program, for example, provides $75 worth of materials to FFN caregivers for completion of its Level 1 training and an additional $100 for completion of Level 2. FFN caregivers participating in Michigan's FUTURES initiative receive a $150 bonus as a reward for completing 15 hours of training. In Kansas, FFN caregivers who complete training offered through the Kansas Relative Care pilot program receive $100 in materials as well as a 10-cent increase in their reimbursement rate (Porter & Kearns, 2005).

EFFORTS SPECIFIC TO PROGRAM TYPES

A second category of tier two efforts to improve the ECE teaching workforce are those established for specific types of ECE programs (i.e., Head Start, prekindergarten, and military child care). What is both interesting and concerning is that nearly every major type of ECE program has undertaken its own integrated effort to address workforce issues—interesting because these efforts highlight the universal need for greater teacher support, and concerning because each endeavor is distinct and often unrelated to the workforce enhancement efforts specific to other program types.

Head Start

Since its inception, Head Start, the nation's major comprehensive child development and family support program for low-income families, has had a deep commitment to workforce enhancement. It has demonstrated sustained commitment to increasing parents' and teachers' access to professional development, supporting workforce diversity, increasing compensation, and improving program directors' managerial skills. For example, early in its history, Head Start was instrumental in the conceptualization and formation of the Child Development Associate Program, the nation's largest and most prominent individual credential that spans all segments of the ECE field.

A strong commitment to professional development and workforce enhancement continues to characterize Head Start, with much of Head Start's commitment to the workforce funded by a required minimum 2% of the entire Head Start budget set aside for training and technical assistance. These funds support multiple efforts that include, but are not limited to, the National Head Start Training and Technical Assistance Resource Centers that support the efforts of regional Training/Technical Assistance and State Collaboration Networks. Other illustrative efforts to enhance professional development include Head Start's Higher Education Partnership, including the: (1) Historically Black College and University (HBCU) Partnerships, (2) Higher Education Hispanic/Latino Service Partnerships, and (3) Head Start Tribally Controlled Land Grant College and University (TCU) Partnerships. These grants enable institutions of higher education to form partnerships with local Head Start programs to enhance teachers' access to training and education. The grantees, then, have the experience and capability to prepare ECE professionals for effective work with linguistically and culturally diverse young children and families. One partnership with an HBCU in South Carolina, for example, focused on recruiting Head Start teachers into bachelor's and master's degree programs. Between 1997 and 2001, this project graduated 14 Head Start staff members, six with a bachelor's degree and eight with a master's degree in early childhood education (Brown, 2002).

At the local level, Head Start programs are required to use portions of their funding to increase quality enhancement efforts, including increasing staff salaries and teachers' professional qualifications, and providing professional development. Regional technical assistance contractors work with local programs to identify quality improvement, training, and technical assistance needs. Local Head Start programs then design technical assistance plans and draw from a bevy of resources that best match their needs. They might, for example, elect to send the program's director to the Johnson & Johnson Management Fellows Program to participate in a 2-week intensive management training session at the UCLA Anderson School of Management. The curriculum focuses on building both executive and entrepreneurial management skills, as well as applying these concepts to relevant Head Start needs and interests. Alternatively, local Head Start programs might elect to avail themselves of other training efforts, including participation in HeadsUp! Reading, a research-based, college-level course on early literacy, or in the National Head Start Association's Webinars, web-based seminars offered on topics pertinent to the Head Start community. Professional development opportunities within Head Start are robust and often are emulated as models of workforce enhancement strategies.

Prekindergarten

The growth of state-funded prekindergarten programs has dramatically expanded ECE opportunities for 3- and 4-year-old children and provided new career opportunities for ECE teachers. As prekindergarten initiatives often function independent of states' child care efforts, many states institute independent policies and practices to address prekindergarten teachers' professional development and compensation.

Prekindergarten programs promote professional development in multiple ways, many of which stem from their close ties to K–12 public school systems. First, prekindergarten teachers typically are required to have professional credentials commensurate with those of teachers in K–12 classrooms. Across the board, these requirements are more stringent than those with which teachers in licensed child care must comply. Second, and not surprising, the greater professional qualifications of prekindergarten teachers are associated with higher levels of compensation than those received by ECE teachers in other settings (Montilla, Twombly, & De Vita, 2001). Third, as public school employees, many prekindergarten teachers may be union members and therefore receive the benefits of contract negotiations that lead to even greater compensation. In the District of Columbia, for example, prekindergarten programs are operated by public schools and are available in all elementary schools across the city. Funding for prekindergarten is provided through the school funding formula and, as a result, prekindergarten teachers' professional qualifications are recognized and rewarded with compensation consistent with that of teachers in the public K–12 education system.

Integrated efforts to address workforce issues in state-funded prekindergarten programs are relatively straightforward in locales where the programs are delivered only in school-based settings. In most states and communities, however, state-funded prekindergarten programs allow children to be served in both public schools and community-based programs (Schumacher, Ewen, Hart, & Lombardi, 2005). In such cases, there are administrative challenges and equity dilemmas; for example, since compensation differs greatly between these two types of ECE programs, teachers in the same program, doing the same work, may be compensated differently. As a consequence, because school-related programs typically have higher wages, better benefits, and more professional development opportunities, many of the highly qualified ECE teachers in community-based programs leave their positions to take ECE jobs in the public schools, jeopardizing the quality of services provided in community-based settings (Whitebook & Sakai, 2003). Most state-funded prekindergarten efforts have not taken steps to minimize these inequities.

Georgia, however, has begun to equalize funding for prekindergarten programs across public and private settings by establishing a base salary for all certified lead teachers; lead prekindergarten teachers earn certification from the Professional Standards Commission, the same body that certifies K–12 teachers (Bright from the Start, 2006). The promise of receiving the same compensation as teachers in the K–12 system, based on the state's Department of Education's salary scale, has provided prekindergarten teachers in community-based settings with an incentive to pursue bachelor's degrees and certification; as a result, 80% of prekindergarten teachers in Georgia now have a BA (Walsh, Graham, & Baker, 2004). Despite this attention to compensation, however, only public schools—not community-based programs—receive additional funds from the state to pay for professional development for certified lead teachers (M. Rieck, personal communication, January 2006).

Military Child Care

The U.S. Department of Defense (DoD) Child Development Program takes a thorough approach to enhancing its ECE workforce (Campbell, Applebaum, Martinson, & Martin, 2000; De Vita & Montilla, 2003). Based on the recognition that soldiers who are concerned about their children's ECE arrangements are less effective on the job, the DoD launched integrated efforts to improve the quality of ECE provided to the children of military personnel on military installations. Congress passed the Military Child Care Act (MCCA) in 1989 to launch a major overhaul of the system. To implement the MCCA, the DoD pursued several strategies, three of which directly affect the workforce: (1) improving accountability through a stringent inspection and certification system, (2) adopting program accreditation and encouraging programs to become accredited, and (3) improving teachers' compensation and training (Campbell et al., 2000).

These strategies affect ECE teachers in many ways. First, the certification standards require all teachers to have a high school diploma, complete 36 hours of training within the first 6 months of child care employment, and thereafter complete 24 hours of training annually. Second, the DoD uses NAEYC accreditation standards for center-based programs. These standards mandate that all teachers have a minimum of an associate's degree and 75% of teachers have a bachelor's degree. FCC providers are encouraged, but not required, to be accredited by NAFCC. Third, to incentivize teachers to pursue training and formal education, the DoD has a wage scale that ties wages to training, education, and performance (Department of Defense, n.d.). Further, once employed by the DoD, ECE teachers have opportunities for career growth through ongoing professional development, including individualized coaching and mentorship. Every DoD center-based program has an education director responsible for enhancing ECE teachers' skills (Ackerman, 2006). To encourage stability of the ECE teaching workforce, teachers who stay within the DoD's child care system receive increases in their compensation. Today, the Military Child Care Act is a model for improving the competence and compensation of ECE teachers. These reform efforts are ongoing, as the DoD continues to invest in certification, accreditation, staff compensation, and training (Pomper, Blank, Campbell, & Schulman, 2005).

More than a decade after the MCCA was passed, evaluations of the reform indicate that it has positively affected military ECE teachers' wages, professional development, and job stability (Campbell et al., 2000; Pomper et al., 2005). Specifically, entry-level salaries increased by an average of almost $2 per hour across all branches of the military, and turnover among ECE teachers decreased from 48% to 23.6%. The quality of military ECE improved because teachers who were less inclined to complete the new requirements left their teaching positions. Vacancies were filled by teachers with formal education and more years of experience who were attracted to the DoD's well-compensated job opportunities (Zellman & Johansen in Park-Jadotte et al., 2002).

Funding for teacher compensation and support is a key ingredient of the program's success. In considering the DoD's impressive progress, it is important to mention how this system is financed. Currently, approximately 50% of the funding to support MCCA comes from third-party sources, either the federal government or the military base that offers the child care. Therefore, parents rarely pay more than 50% of the cost of this high-quality care (Zellman & Gates, 2002).

UNIONIZATION

Unionization is the third major category of integrated efforts, situated in tier two of the pyramid, to enhance the competence and stability of the ECE teaching workforce. Typically, unionization uses multiple strategies to improve both teachers' compensation and working conditions. In contrast to many conventional top-down ECE workforce efforts, it represents bottom-up reform because it relies on the collective voices and votes of individual ECE teachers. Examples of the power of unionization to increase ECE teachers' compensation are numerous. In 1999, for example, the

Confederation of National Trade Unions in Quebec won substantial increases in ECE teachers' wages along with greater public support for child care (Folbre, 2006). In Washington State, some attribute the development of the statewide Early Childhood Education Career and Wage Ladder Pilot Project to the successful organization of ECE teachers by the local union. Launched in 2000, and discussed in greater detail earlier in this chapter, Washington's Career and Wage Ladder utilized public and private resources to increase the wages of approximately 1,500 teachers in 117 ECE programs (Moon & Burbank, 2004). Although the project was discontinued in 2003 because of budget cuts, it demonstrates how unions can work in partnership with the government and private agencies to increase teachers' compensation.

Unionization is increasingly popular among FCC providers as a mechanism to increase compensation and job satisfaction. Indeed, unions in several states are reaching out to FCC providers. In 2005, Illinois became the first state to grant collective bargaining rights to FCC providers (Service Employees International Union, 2005). FCC providers in that state joined the union to redress low pay, long hours, and lack of health insurance or benefits. As a result of joining the union, FCC providers report feeling greater respect and less isolation. One analysis of Illinois's efforts suggests that unionization also can have a positive impact on the quality of ECE by building public and consumer support for investing in high-quality ECE (Brooks, 2005). More recently, unions in Washington State and Iowa have made progress in organizing FCC providers to improve compensation.

As with other efforts to raise ECE teachers' compensation, unionization requires an increase in funding. To generate that funding, either families or the government must increase expenditures for ECE. Instead of paying the higher cost, the government may decrease the number of subsidies available to families, or families may choose less expensive ECE programs for their children. Both of these scenarios may decrease the supply of ECE, which could adversely impact teachers, children, and families. Thus, union efforts incur some of the spillover effects discussed in Chapter 5 and should be considered carefully in light of potential unintended consequences.

COLLECTIVE MANAGEMENT AND SHARED SERVICES

The fourth category of tier two integrated efforts encompasses collective management and shared services strategies. These efforts unite independent ECE programs and thereby capitalize on economies of scale. Aggregation leads to better benefits and workplace environments for ECE teachers, two important factors that contribute to a more competent and stable workforce.

Stoney (2004a) describes four primary types of collective management and shared services arrangements: (1) multisite ECE programs, formed when one corporate entity operates multiple center-based sites; (2) ECE program alliances, in which independent child care centers form ECE program partnerships to share some management functions; (3) home-based ECE alliances, comprising independent businesses that share all or some of the financial and management functions involved in providing home-based ECE; and (4) support services alliances, in which independent child care centers or FCC providers contract with a single entity to provide some management support services such as staffing, recruiting and hiring substitutes, or food preparation/management. These four types of collective management and shared services arrangements address multiple workforce conditions: professional development, compensation, and/or the work environment. In order to succeed, collective management requires a shared vision and strong leadership; in other words, "the whole must be greater than the sum of its parts" (Stoney, 2004a, p. 28).

With collective management and shared services strategies, programs may access the many benefits of group negotiations, collective administration, and purchasing. In addition, programs that engage in collective management may find that participation promotes more stable and responsive work environments. With a larger pool of employees, for example, substitute teachers may be available when a teacher is away from work tending to personal needs or pursuing professional development opportunities. Similarly, ECE programs that merge administrative functions benefit from more efficient management, budgeting, rate setting, and payment collection (Stoney, 2004a). Collective management also enables programs to offer more comprehensive employee benefits—including full health and dental coverage, pension plans, and paid vacations, sick days, and personal days—than individual programs are able to provide alone.

Collective management is a particularly relevant strategy for family child care providers because it transcends existing FCC cost- and labor-consolidation efforts. Family Child Care Networks provide individualized professional development opportunities and may assume responsibility for some of providers' administrative obligations (Hamm et al., 2005). Shared services alliances go one step further in that they enable participating FCC providers to engage a third party to manage laborious and costly administrative functions. In particular, alliances process payments more effectively and efficiently for FCC providers. Alliances also may facilitate enrollment in FCC programs so that providers can care for the maximum number of children. These supportive services translate into greater income for generally underpaid FCC providers (Stoney, 2004a).

CONCLUSION

In this chapter we have discussed tier two, or integrated, efforts that address multiple challenges faced by the ECE workforce. Efforts in this tier acknowledge the interconnectedness of professional development, compensation, and work environment. Integrated efforts that aim to improve both compensation and professional qualifications, for example, avoid the "chicken or egg" conundrum of whether increased compensation leads to the ability to recruit and retain teachers with higher qualifications, or whether requiring ECE teachers to have higher qualifications allows them to justify and command higher compensation. Indeed, there are a number of exemplary program-specific efforts that systematically support ECE teacher quality by establishing teacher requirements that exceed child care regulations, offering a range of supportive ongoing professional development opportunities, and rewarding teachers who have attained higher levels of education with higher compensation. Yet, existing efforts that link compensation and professional development, enhance quality in specific programs or program types, or promote unionization and collective management are limited to certain types of ECE programs or to ECE teachers in certain geographic localities. Thus, we have ample examples of strategies currently supporting *some* ECE teachers that could be scaled up to support *all* ECE teachers.

Although the policies and programs discussed in this chapter provide integrated, comprehensive support to strengthen and improve portions of the ECE workforce, improving the entire workforce ultimately rests on the strength of more systemic efforts. To support all ECE teachers equitably, fully, and sustainably, there must be policies and programs that align and integrate all workforce-related efforts within a comprehensive and coherent system. In the next chapter, we turn to tier three with a discussion of these systemic policies and programs.

Tier Three: Systems and Systemic Efforts

IN THE LAST chapter, we discussed integrated efforts directly related to improving the quality of the ECE teaching workforce. These efforts were characterized by two properties: First, they were directly targeted at the ECE teaching workforce itself; and second, although each addressed multiple challenges simultaneously, none addressed all components necessary to reform the workforce. In this chapter, we turn to a discussion of efforts that are broader than any presented thus far. We use the term *broader* in two ways. First, they are comprehensive and encompass a range of strategies and efforts that systematically embrace and align all of the essential elements necessary to support a high-quality workforce. To that end, we begin this chapter with a discussion of professional development systems. Second, some of the most important efforts to improve the ECE workforce do not present themselves as efforts to improve the teaching workforce per se. Transcending the ECE workforce, these efforts aim to foster the development of the early childhood system. Some of the efforts focus on comprehensive approaches to program quality improvement; others focus on building public will and parental knowledge, and still others work to strengthen the early childhood system through inventive financing mechanisms. In each case, however, the efforts heavily impact the ECE workforce, reinforcing its pivotal place in the early childhood system. In this chapter, then, we address efforts that support comprehensive professional development systems and those that aim to build the early childhood system; we do so in four sections: (1) professional development systems, (2) broad program quality improvement efforts, (3) public and parental information efforts, and (4) comprehensive funding efforts.

PROFESSIONAL DEVELOPMENT SYSTEMS

As their name suggests, professional development systems (PDSs) are predicated on a commitment to systemic reform. PDSs build the infrastructure necessary to ensure that all ECE teachers have access to an integrated system of professional development that links training and formal education, addresses the content and quality of training through a quality approval process, provides incentives (including compensation) for training, and offers training passports or career registries that chronicle the cumulative training and education individuals receive. Most PDSs seek to reduce discrepancies in access to professional development by providing support for all teachers, regardless of the setting in which they work. In this sense, ideal professional development systems are not targeted to one program type, but embrace diverse ECE sectors (e.g., child care, prekindergarten, Head Start) to streamline expectations and opportunities for all ECE teachers and directors.

In 2005, 38 states were building professional development systems (LeMoine as part of a presentation of the Workgroup on Defining and Measuring Early Childhood Professional Development, 2005). Despite the prevalence of PDS efforts, no two states are alike in their approach to this work. They are alike, however, in that few states have achieved a fully functioning professional development system. In large part, this is because PDS efforts have very broad goals and these efforts are constantly evolving as the ECE landscape changes. To support states in creating comprehensive PDSs, the National Child Care Information Center (NCCIC) (2006b) identified "Elements of a Professional Development System for Early Care and Education: A Simplified Framework and Definitions." This framework outlines five elements of a PDS: (1) access and outreach, (2) qualifications and credentials, (3) quality assurances, (4) core knowledge, and (5) funding. NCCIC also documents states' efforts within these five categories, noting that all 50 states have made some effort in one of these five broad categories and 21 states have policies and practices in all five areas.

Others proffer an alternative structure for a comprehensive PDS, providing a different framework to consider the vital elements of a system of workforce improvement. Kagan, Tarrant, and Berliner (2005) identify 10 elements that constitute a comprehensive professional development system:

1. *Core knowledge.* The range of knowledge and observable skills that adults working with young children need in order to facilitate children's learning and development.
2. *Career path.* Also known as a "career lattice" or "career ladder," the continuum of levels of mastery that reflect workers' experience, training, and educational accomplishments. Career paths exist for a variety of direct service roles in the field (e.g., teachers, administrators, and family child care providers).
3. *Professional development delivery mechanism.* The coordination of training and education among the multiple institutions that offer training and formal education.
4. *Quality approval and assurance system.* A process for evaluating the training and education ECE teachers may apply toward advancement

in their career paths. Often, a state will establish an entity to monitor the quality of training, calling it a "Training Quality Approval System" or a "Training Quality Assurance Board." This entity reviews the content of training to determine its relation to the state's core knowledge areas; it also may register and assess the quality of individual trainers.

5. *Qualifications and credentials.* Proof of professional training and/or experience that ECE teachers achieve as they advance in the career path, including entry requirements, ongoing requirements, and credentials. "Career registries" or "professional development records" often are used to document teachers' qualifications and credentials.

6. *Incentives for professional development.* Financial and other awards that encourage ECE teachers to advance professionally, including scholarships for professional development, compensation increases tied to higher professional qualifications, and acknowledgment of excellence in ECE teaching.

7. *Access and outreach.* Efforts to publicize information about a PDS to encourage and facilitate ECE teachers' participation in the opportunities the system offers.

8. *Financing.* The revenue generation and deployment strategies used to finance a professional development system. This element of a PDS is linked to the overall financing for an ECE system but specifically addresses funding for professional development.

9. *Governance.* The processes by which policy, fiscal, and administrative decisions are rendered and enforced. Governance of a PDS is related to the overall governance of the ECE system.

10. *Evaluation.* A process that is built into the overall PDS, and/or each element thereof, to determine its success in meeting its goals and to provide timely and accurate information to improve the system's performance.

Irrespective of which definition of professional development system one espouses, three key conditions must exist for a PDS to succeed. First, all elements of the PDS must be conceptualized and constructed so that they reinforce one another. Second, the PDS cannot function alone; it must be nested within the broader ECE system. Finally, the PDS must address ECE teachers in all types of programs, in both the public and private sectors. Below, we present comprehensive PDS efforts underway in Pennsylvania and New Mexico, to illustrate how states are successfully implementing professional development systems.

Pennsylvania has an exemplary PDS because, in addition to addressing all 10 elements detailed above, it also reflects the three key conditions. Pennsylvania's core body of knowledge (element 1) serves as the foundation for the PDS. All instructors who are approved by the Pennsylvania quality assurance system (element 4) must be trained on the use of the core body of knowledge. Together, the quality assurance process and core knowledge establish a framework for professional development records (element 5) that document teachers' professional development as they progress through the state's career lattice (element 2). When looking for professional development opportunities, teachers can access professional development through an online training calendar and online system for training registration (element 7). In addition, Pennsylvania has a sophisticated professional development delivery mechanism (element 3) that includes provision of specialized training throughout the state and articulation agreements between many of the state's institutions of higher education that enable teachers to transfer credits from an associate's degree into a bachelor's degree program. Pennsylvania offers incentives for teachers to pursue specialized formal education and training through a loan forgiveness program, free training, professional development vouchers, T.E.A.C.H. Early Childhood® scholarships, and education and retention grants for programs that hire highly qualified teachers (element 6). Pennsylvania finances the professional development system through a combination of federal, state, and philanthropic funds (element 8), and it has developed so-called Regional Keys, geographically dispersed organizations that govern, plan, and deliver training to meet the needs of ECE teachers in different areas of the state (element 9). Moreover, Pennsylvania has coordinated its PDS with the larger ECE system; for example, the regional organizations that govern and implement both the PDS and the state's quality rating system also work in close partnership with the state's Office of Child Development and Early Learning, the executive-level state office that integrates child care and early education programs. Unlike many other states, Pennsylvania has evaluated its PDS and used the results of these evaluations to improve support for ECE teachers (element 10) (Office of Child Development, 2006).

For PDSs to improve the overall quality of the ECE teaching workforce, they must include and address each sector of the ECE system. In New Mexico, for example, teachers in Head Start, child care, preschool special education, and public prekindergarten through 3rd-grade programs all have access to the state's professional development system. To accomplish this, New Mexico's Office of Child Development in the Department of Children, Youth, and Families (CYF) collaborates closely with the state's

Department of Education (DOE) to offer a unified credentialing process; the former grants early childhood credentials to ECE teachers with associate's degrees or below, while the latter licenses all ECE teachers who have bachelor's degrees or above (element 5). The CYF credential and DOE license are rungs on the state's career ladder (element 2), which applies to all ECE teachers, regardless of the setting in which they work (Mitchell & LeMoine, 2005). In addition to its career path, New Mexico's PDS has most of the aforementioned 10 elements. Its core knowledge (element 1) forms the basis of its professional development delivery mechanism (element 3), which includes a universal catalog of courses encompassing ECE program offerings at all 2- and 4-year institutions throughout the state. To encourage teachers to pursue higher education (element 6), New Mexico offers T.E.A.C.H. Early Childhood® scholarships to ECE teachers. The Office of Child Development, the entity responsible for the PDS (element 9), is funded with state general resources; the full PDS, however, relies on state, federal, and private funding from each sector (element 8). New Mexico has not yet evaluated its PDS (element 10).

PROGRAM QUALITY IMPROVEMENT EFFORTS

Program quality improvement efforts embrace multiple dimensions of the infrastructure and direct services that constitute a comprehensive ECE system. Specifically, these efforts address teacher quality and program quality together, as interdependent facets of an ECE system. Two primary mechanisms have been used to improve the overall quality of ECE: (1) program accreditation, and (2) quality rating systems (QRSs). While accreditation is usually a private enterprise and QRSs are predominantly a public enterprise, they are highly interrelated. Both define standards—for the workforce and the programs themselves—for high-quality early care and education. QRSs differ from accreditation in that they define several different levels of standards, each of which serves as a stepping stone to higher levels of quality. By comparison, accreditation defines a single level of quality, but it is often the highest level of quality recognized by QRSs. As such, QRSs and accreditation work in tandem to improve the quality of young children's ECE arrangements, including the quality of their ECE teachers.

Accreditation

Accreditation is a voluntary process whereby ECE programs self-assess their overall quality, including the qualifications and competence of their workforce. External raters visit programs to ensure the accuracy of the self-assessment. The raters' reports are submitted to a national body of experts who determine whether the program qualifies for accreditation. The criteria for accreditation are diverse (e.g., standards exist for issues ranging from curricula to community relationships), but they always include elements related to professional development and specific requirements for ECE teachers' qualifications. As such, accreditation is not exclusively focused on, but has a direct and important impact on, the ECE workforce.

Several associations have developed accreditation procedures and criteria to evaluate the quality of ECE programs. For center-based ECE programs, the National Association for the Education of Young Children (NAEYC) administers a highly respected and rigorous assessment that most states consider the gold standard for program quality. Many states also recognize the National Association of Family Child Care (NAFCC) accreditation for FCC providers. The impact of accreditation on program quality and children's developmental outcomes has been evaluated at both the national and state level. One study of NAEYC accreditation in Minnesota, for example, found that accreditation improved both the quality of programs and the quality of teachers, contributing to better child outcomes (Minnesota Department of Human Services, 2005). Nearly twice as many children in accredited centers were rated ready for school when compared with children statewide. In particular, children from lower income families in accredited centers had much higher average proficiency scores than the statewide pool of their peers. Positive effects of accreditation also were found in California, where NAEYC-accredited centers rated higher on measures of teacher sensitivity than centers that began the accreditation process but did not achieve it (Whitebook et al., 1997). Data from a national study show that NAEYC accreditation is associated with teachers' compensation, finding that accredited centers' wages are 9.5% to 33.7% higher than those of nonaccredited centers, depending on job category (Whitebook et al., 1998). Together, these studies suggest that accreditation is a powerful tool for improving important aspects of the ECE system (i.e., program quality and teacher compensation) and, therefore, child outcomes.

Quality Rating Systems

Many states have developed quality rating systems (QRSs) to induce ECE programs to improve their quality, including the quality of their teachers. QRSs typically are publicly supported efforts to gauge ECE program quality based on factors such as classroom quality assessments, staff qualifications, and administrative procedures. As of 2007, 13 states and the District of Columbia, along with several communities throughout the country, had adopted QRSs (National Child Care Information Center, 2007). Not all QRSs are the same, however. The most comprehensive efforts cover center-based child care, family child care, after-school care, prekindergarten programs, and Head Start (Mitchell, 2005); some states' efforts embrace only a few of these program types. While each QRS has unique characteristics, they generally share three primary goals: (1) improving the overall quality of ECE programs, (2) raising public and consumer awareness about program quality, and (3) providing increased funding to encourage and reward programs that provide higher quality ECE. Because teacher quality is central to program quality, each of these three goals directly and indirectly affects the ECE teaching workforce. Only one state, Tennessee, makes participation in the QRS mandatory, while the other states offer it on a voluntary basis. Some states offer higher reimbursements through the child care subsidy system or other financial awards to participating ECE programs that provide higher quality ECE. Some states establish a QRS in statute, while others do so in agency regulations (Mitchell, 2005).

Central to QRSs is the focus on overall quality improvement. States adopt rating scales, usually using stars as the metric, with a greater number of stars indicating a higher quality program. ECE programs usually are required to display their rating for parents, staff, and the public to see. In North Carolina, for example, programs receive a QRS certificate that has the outline of five stars; one star is filled in for each level of quality that the program achieves. In this way, anyone looking at the certificate knows what constitutes high quality (five stars) and where the program currently ranks. Other states post program quality information on publicly accessible websites, allowing parents to review all pertinent facets of each ECE program. These resources provide crucial guidance to parents who are "shopping" for programs for their children, and they also inform the general public about quality enhancement efforts. As a result, they advance public accountability.

In pioneering the star-rated license, North Carolina was one of the first states to develop a quality rating system for ECE programs statewide, recognizing both center-based programs and FCC homes for their program standards and staff education. The North Carolina system relies on state-trained evaluators, who visit programs and use environment rating scales to assess the quality of care children receive. The state's Smart Start initiative then offers technical assistance to help programs attain higher ratings. In fact, local Smart Start partnerships are responsible for increasing the number of programs at higher rating levels (Mitchell, 2005). As a result of this QRS, North Carolina can promote systematic improvement in its overall ECE quality. One study found that center-based programs with higher scores on the state's quality rating system had large proportions of teachers whose classroom practices benefited children's learning and development (de Kruif et al., 2000). These results show that program and teacher quality, together, make a difference.

Learning from North Carolina and other states' QRSs, Pennsylvania launched its QRS, Keystone Stars Child Care Quality Initiative (Keystone Stars) in 2002. Keystone Stars rates programs based on the quality of staff education, the ECE program environment, partnerships with families and community, and leadership and management; a designation of four stars represents the highest quality rating (Office of Child Development, 2006). To help programs adopt higher quality practices, regional offices assess programs' quality, create quality improvement plans with program administrators, and provide intensive, one-on-one technical assistance. Importantly, Keystone Stars provides substantial funding to encourage programs to achieve the next star level. Support grants ranging from $750 (for a one-star FCC home) to $12,000 (for a large three-star center) are awarded to programs upon certification of an increased star designation (Mitchell, 2005). In addition, programs that maintain high quality over time are eligible to receive annual Stars Merit Awards that range from $800 (for a two-star FCC home) to $54,000 (for a large four-star center). To emphasize the importance of teacher quality, Keystone Stars offers teacher education and retention awards for programs with ratings of two stars or higher (Stoney, 2004b). Furthermore, when reviewing applicants to its T.E.A.C.H. Early Childhood® program, Pennsylvania gives higher priority to ECE teachers working in two-star or higher rated programs (Stoney, 2004b). Therefore, enhancing teacher quality is considered integral to Pennsylvania's broader goal, and the goal of QRSs in general, of enhancing the overall quality of ECE.

PUBLIC/PARENTAL INFORMATION ABOUT ECE QUALITY

Program quality enhancement efforts are effective in building a *system* of early care and education only to the extent they meet the needs of their consumers (families and children). Public awareness and parental information efforts help increase consumer demand for high-quality ECE programs by conveying two critical messages: (1) that high-quality programs are more desirable because they are better for children, and (2) that high-quality teachers go hand-in-hand with higher quality programs. If parents demand higher quality programs with more qualified teachers, ECE programs will be forced to hire and train such personnel or face the prospects of parents' taking their "business" elsewhere. Sometimes public awareness efforts make explicit reference to the importance of the workforce; sometimes they do not. Whether explicit or implicit, references to ECE teachers are the subtext of these public awareness efforts. They acknowledge that good results do not occur unless ECE programs are of high quality, and that high-quality ECE programs cannot exist without competent teachers. Therefore, better information may promote teachers' professional development and, in turn, enhance compensation.

Conceptually, parental information efforts go one step further than public awareness campaigns. As noted in Chapter 5, market failure stems from consumers' inability to discern quality. If the elements of quality or a specific quality rating was understood by consumers, the market could move closer to equilibrium. All things being equal, parents would opt for high-quality settings for their children, accelerating competition among providers. Such competition would attract teachers and professionals with higher qualifications or greater competence to programs offering a better work environment and greater compensation. While far from functioning perfectly, the ECE market might reward better programs if parents were more aware of quality indicators and their implications.

Child Care Resource and Referral (CCR&R) agencies provide the most intentional and systematic information about ECE quality to policymakers and parents. Over the past several years, partnerships between CCR&Rs and QRSs have begun to emerge in states, providing even more specific and meaningful information about ECE teacher and program quality.

Child Care Resource and Referral

Child Care Resource and Referral agencies have been established throughout the country to help parents find child care and to improve the quality of ECE programs. In 2002, the National Association of Child Care Resource and Referral Agencies established criteria for CCR&Rs' parent referral services to ensure that these agencies provide parents with accurate and meaningful information about ECE programs. The first of these criteria is that referral services be provided directly to families through multiple channels (e.g., telephone, face-to-face, Internet, and written materials). The second criterion is that each CCR&R have a current and complete database of referral information, including information about the availability, affordability, and basic quality of a variety of ECE programs. This criterion addresses the capacity of CCR&Rs to help families access ECE programs that meet families' multiple and diverse needs. The third criterion, fostering community engagement, encourages CCR&Rs to improve public awareness and utilization of CCR&R services (Consumer Education Quality Assurance Program, 2002).

Combining Quality Rating Systems and Child Care Resource and Referral Agencies

While Child Care Resource and Referral Agencies alone are equipped to convey basic information about the availability and quality of ECE programs, quality rating systems (QRSs) convey more detailed and nuanced information about the quality of one program compared with other programs, including information about teachers' qualifications (Mitchell, 2005). When CCR&Rs join forces with QRSs, parents can easily access in-depth information about ECE quality to make more informed choices about their children's early care and education arrangements. Although not all CCR&Rs have partnered with QRSs, all QRSs have established partnerships with CCR&Rs (Mitchell, 2005).

Colorado's Qualistar Early Learning organization, for example, merged the state's QRS with the statewide network of CCR&R agencies to provide consumers with information about the quality of ECE programs available throughout the state. Parents and others looking for an ECE program may visit Qualistar's website and generate a list of ECE programs in their community; the list provides each program's address, phone number, quality star rating, and an early learning report that summarizes the program's rating evaluations and recommendations for quality improvement (Qualistar, 2004). Early results of the program's evaluation suggest that Qualistar's QRS has improved the quality of participating ECE programs and, to a moderate extent, the quality of teacher–child interactions (G. Westervelt, personal communication, February 2006). This evaluation ultimately will assess the relationship between program quality and child outcomes (D. Schaack, personal communication, March 2006). Although the results are preliminary, partnerships between QRSs and CCR&Rs may improve outcomes not only for program quality, but also for ECE teachers and young children.

COMPREHENSIVE FUNDING EFFORTS

Both professional development systems and quality rating systems require sufficient and sustainable funding. In the absence of adequate financial resources, these program quality enhancement efforts will have only limited effect—either because only some parents and families will be able to afford the higher costs of high-quality ECE (thereby defeating the goal of ensuring that *all* children, *all* families, and *all* ECE teachers benefit) or because the systems themselves will collapse from fragile, insubstantial, and underfunded infrastructure. Increasing public investments in the ECE system is crucial. Two promising approaches to ECE funding have the potential to sustain broad and systemic reforms on behalf of the ECE workforce: (1) offering financial incentives for higher quality care, and (2) financing a high-quality ECE system.

Financial Incentives for Higher Quality Care

As noted throughout this volume, efforts to improve the ECE workforce are costly to implement. States use several strategies to provide financial incentives for improving the quality of ECE. Financial incentives operate through two distinct mechanisms: (1) direct funding for ECE programs themselves to improve quality, or (2) subsidies for parents to select higher quality ECE. Because high-quality teachers lie at the heart of high-quality programs, both types of incentives indirectly aim to increase the demand for high-quality teachers.

Financial Incentives for Programs to Improve Quality. Both tiered child care subsidy reimbursements and merit grants that reward the achievement and maintenance of quality provide direct incentives to ECE programs to improve quality. Thirty states have implemented tiered reimbursement systems that provide higher child care subsidy reimbursement rates to ECE programs that achieve quality beyond licensing requirements, as evidenced, for example, through achieving accreditation (National Association for the Education of Young Children, 2006b). In 2006, 10 of the 14 statewide quality rating systems (including that of the District of Columbia) provided higher subsidy reimbursements for children who received child care subsidies, to reward ECE programs that deliver higher levels of quality (National Child Care Information Center, 2006a). Assuming that high-quality programs employ and support teachers with higher qualifications, tiered reimbursement strengthens the ECE teaching workforce by rewarding programs that invest in their teachers' education and training. The programs, in turn, may use the increased reimbursements to increase their potential pool of funds for paying teachers' salaries.

While tiered subsidy reimbursement provides incentives for programs to improve their quality, it provides only marginal increases to programs' overall revenue, which may limit the capacity for programs to invest substantially in their teachers' professional development or compensation. Moreover, because tiered reimbursement rate ceilings are tied to the market rate, this strategy may have the adverse effect of driving up the cost of care for private fee-paying families. In addition, tiered subsidy reimbursement policies provide incentives only for those programs that serve children eligible to receive subsidies. Thus, financial incentives via child care subsidy reimbursements have limited capacity to improve the quality of *all* ECE programs and teachers.

Unlike tiered subsidy reimbursements that function through the child care subsidy system, awards and grants that reward higher quality need not be directly linked to a particular funding stream or sector. Quality awards and grants, therefore, have the potential to broadly impact the ECE field; they can be provided directly to ECE programs—*all* programs—based on the level of quality care and education provided.

To illustrate, Pennsylvania's QRS, Keystone Stars, rewards all types of high-quality ECE programs with merit awards and grants. It is distinct from the state's licensing process, and there is no relationship between higher star ratings and child care subsidy reimbursements from the state Department of Public Welfare. Therefore, Pennsylvania's quality awards apply to all types of ECE programs serving young children, not just those that care for children eligible for child care subsidy. Because Keystone Stars' merit awards are generous (up to $54,000 for very high-quality large center-based programs), ECE programs are able to invest significant resources in their teachers (Mitchell, 2005).

Financial Incentives to Parents Who Select Higher Quality Care. Another way to encourage ECE quality improvement is by providing financial incentives to parents and families who enroll their children in programs with higher quality, thereby increasing the demand for high-quality programs. States' tax policies, specifically their tax credit policies, are a mechanism for doing this. If a family pays someone else to care for its children, tax credits can reduce the amount of taxes paid by the family; the credit amount is usually a percentage of the amount of related expenses paid to an ECE program or provider. Some tax credits incentivize higher quality by adding a stipulation that the ECE program or provider have a verifiable level of quality achievement.

States with tax credits linked to the federal dependent care tax credit encourage parents to choose high-quality ECE. For example, Maine links the amount of its state tax credit to stringent ECE program quality requirements; parents who choose high-quality ECE are eligible for a double child care tax credit on their state income tax return. High-quality programs must have a quality certificate, documenting that they meet minimum licensing standards and are accredited by an independent, nationally recognized organization approved by the Maine Department of Human Services, Office of Head Start and Child Care. In addition, for an ECE program to earn a quality certificate, its policies, procedures, and program records are analyzed and the program itself is subject to an on-site review (Donahue &

Campbell, 2002). Parents who choose high-quality FCC providers are also eligible to receive the tax credit. FCC providers who have Child Development Associate credentials or associate's, bachelor's, master's, or doctoral degrees in early childhood education, child development, or a related field are considered to be of high quality (Maine Department of Health and Human Services Office of Child Care and Head Start, 2005).

Financing a High-Quality ECE System: Assessing and Paying the Full Cost of Quality

Any corporate CEO or organizational finance director knows the importance of having a budget that estimates the cost of doing business. Budgets usually include estimates for the costs associated with facilities, personnel, and other operational needs. Knowing what projected costs are associated with doing business helps organizations both plan for how much revenue and resources will be needed in the short term and anticipate the costs of future business growth over the long term. Increasingly, the ECE field is recognizing that in order to be strategic and realistic about implementation, it is crucial to understand the costs associated with systemic efforts to improve ECE quality. Not unlike organizational budgeting, therefore, efforts to estimate the costs of implementing a system of high-quality ECE have been launched. Just like budgeting in any other service-related industry, estimates of the full costs of an ECE system consider how much money will be needed to both recruit and retain personnel who can provide high-quality services. In this sense, the costs associated with providing high-quality professional development, compensation, and work environments are inseparable. Mitchell and Stoney (2004) reiterate the importance of considering standards for teachers' qualifications when reforming the financing of ECE; these standards define essential cost parameters for the overall system.

Beginning with the Cost, Quality, and Outcomes study in 1995, researchers measured the cost of then-current ECE programs and used those data to estimate the cost of creating a high-quality ECE system (Helburn, 1995). In 2002, Helburn and Bergmann estimated that $50 billion would be necessary to provide all families in the United States with access to affordable ECE programs of improved quality. The National Institute for Early Education Research (2003) estimated that approximately $70 billion would be needed to fund universal preschool for America's 3- and 4-year-olds. While the amount required to fully fund a national system of high-quality ECE programs with adequately qualified and compensated teachers depends on the nature of services provided (e.g., full-day or half-day; comprehensive or educational services), substantial additional investment obviously is needed.

To assist policymakers in determining the amount of funding needed to implement a high-quality ECE system, researchers have developed mathematical models that compare the costs of alternative approaches to providing high-quality ECE. Brandon, Kagan, and Joesch (2000) created a model for financing a system of ECE for children birth to age 5, and Golin, Mitchell, and Gault (2004) developed a model to estimate the cost of a statewide preschool program for 3- and 4-year-old children. Because personnel costs constitute a majority of ECE program budgets, both models require policymakers to make important decisions regarding teachers' compensation and qualifications. For example, they must consider how many teachers would be needed, what kind of qualifications they want those teachers to have, and how many teachers would need to improve their qualifications to meet selected standards.

Beyond assessing and estimating the full cost of providing high-quality care, some jurisdictions have tackled the challenge of assessing *and* paying for high-quality care. Kansas City's Metropolitan Council on Child Care assessed the cost of bringing all programs into alignment with NAEYC accreditation standards and adequately compensating all ECE teachers. The council reasoned that if ECE programs were aware, first, of inadequacies in their budgets and, second, that public child care subsidy represents only a portion of what high-quality ECE truly costs, then the programs would be better motivated and equipped to seek additional sources of revenue (Mitchell & Morgan, 2000). With financial support from a local foundation, ECE programs were given the funds to provide high-quality care. Unfortunately, this effort ended when foundation resources were depleted, pointing to the need for sustained funding to maintain quality in ECE.

As the Department of Defense (DoD) overhauled its child care system, policymakers realized that additional resources were needed to offer high-quality ECE programs. In 1990, Congress increased funds for military child care by $128 million. A decade later, about $352 million was earmarked for the DoD's child development program (Campbell et al., 2000), and the investment increased by more than the rate of inflation between FY2000 and FY2005 (Pomper et al., 2005). Within military child care, approximately half of the total cost of care is paid by the DoD, using revenues from military base operations. As a result of this investment in quality, ECE teachers in military child care programs have high levels of formal education, specialized training, compensation, and benefits. In sum, substantial and sustainable funding has enhanced the quality of this segment of the ECE workforce.

CONCLUSION

Systemic efforts to improve the ECE workforce recognize the essential inter-connectedness of quality enhancement; these efforts further recognize that broad-based change requires comprehensive endeavor. Instead of an add-on program here or a one-time initiative there, systemic efforts tackle reform of the infrastructure that supports the ECE workforce—infrastructure such as professional development systems, quality rating systems, political and public will, and financing for a comprehensive system. These efforts can provide the foundation for ensuring that *all* ECE programs are staffed with highly qualified and well-compensated teachers. They clearly articulate standards for professional development, compensation, and work environments. They provide financial incentives to support quality improvement. And they address populations, content, and institutions that have been neglected through decades of haphazard and uncoordinated activities.

Without additional investments in ECE, however, quality improvement initiatives are unlikely to overcome ECE teachers' persistently low wages and low qualifications. Our review shows that successful systemic quality enhancement initiatives, such as the DoD's, rely on the infusion of substantial and sustainable funding into ECE programs. These investments, though, are not likely to be made in all programs without increased political and public awareness and a clearer understanding of how much money is needed and for what purposes the money will be used.

This review of research and existing policies and programs suggests that incentives for ECE program improvement have the potential to improve the quality of the ECE workforce. As such, these broad, systemic efforts play an important role in directly and indirectly enhancing workforce effectiveness.

A Social Strategy: What Should Be Done?

To ADDRESS what should be done in the future, we return to Julius Richmond, to whom this book is dedicated, and his three-faceted model of social change. Richmond applied this model in two successful movements: the establishment of comprehensive child development services, and the smoking cessation movement that changed America's perception of and response to smoking-related illnesses and healthy living. In both cases, he insisted that any major social reform requires three conditions: a solid knowledge base, both wide and deep political and public will, and a compelling social strategy. This volume's structure and substance have followed that trilogy.

Part II of this volume addressed the knowledge base. It provided a comprehensive overview of existing data on the early care and education teaching workforce, including descriptive data about not only *who* constitutes the ECE workforce (Chapter 3) but also *how* ECE teachers perform in the classroom and how effective they are in improving child outcomes (Chapter 4). Transcending the individuals who constitute the workforce, Part II also addressed the institutions that impact the workforce and the systemic challenges that make reform of the ECE workforce complex (Chapter 5). We noted that the challenges include definitional discrepancies as evidenced by the lack of universally accepted definitions and standards of quality teaching. They include structural deficiencies or systemic incompatibilities created by unpredictable investment of resources (both financial and technical) in mixed-sector delivery mechanisms. The challenges also include ideological differences in professional development theories and practices. The knowledge base has shown us that widely variable policies, a fragmented infrastructure, and a highly imperfect market characterize the uniquely American ECE non-system and its workforce.

Part III provided an overview of the nascent and fragmented, yet crucially important, political and public will that exists. This will is evidenced by the many existing programs and efforts that aim to improve the ECE workforce. Some of these have targeted missions, focusing on single components (Chapter 6); others have more integrated missions, linking multiple goals together to improve professional development, compensation, and working conditions for the ECE workforce (Chapter 7); and still others are systemic in nature, taking broad approaches that transcend, yet encompass, the ECE workforce (Chapter 8). These policies and programs to improve the ECE teaching workforce are all noteworthy and necessary. Indeed, they provide a strong launching pad for a new generation of efforts. Yet, these innovative efforts remain largely unconnected within and across tiers; they are not universal, but rather highly idiosyncratic to states and/or program types. Because next-generation efforts must cohere and apply to ECE broadly, strategic policy and research efforts are needed in all three tiers simultaneously.

In Part IV, we address the third condition of the Richmond typology: a social strategy. A social strategy is a plan or blueprint that considers the knowledge base and the status of political and public will, and then renders an analysis of specific, actionable efforts that can improve policies and programs. To that end, in the chapter that follows, we use the information from the preceding parts to proffer a social strategy that will reform the ECE workforce. If the first parts of this volume helped to contextualize where we are—describing the existing knowledge base and political and public will—this part envisions where we want to be and provides substantive recommendations to help us get from here to there.

CHAPTER 9

Recommendations for Reform
of the ECE Teaching Workforce

With the Richmond framework solidly in mind, this chapter presents a social strategy for reforming the ECE teaching workforce. It outlines what we deem a comprehensive, large-scale, and doable set of recommendations. While we envision the following recommendations to be an integrated social strategy, we have divided them into three sections. The first set of recommendations targets improvement of the knowledge base. The second set focuses on strategies that will increase both the political and public will. The third set presents the major structural components of our strategy, setting forth bold new directions for the professional development and compensation of the ECE teaching workforce.

STRATEGIES FOR STRENGTHENING THE KNOWLEDGE BASE

While much is known about the ECE teaching workforce—the characteristics of the individuals who constitute the field, what makes them more effective in the classroom, and the major challenges they face—there is still abundant room to expand and strengthen the knowledge base. The first set of three recommendations in our overall social strategy is framed to address existing gaps in knowledge, expanding both the scientific evidence and the administrative database upon which important decisions about the ECE workforce can be made. As Julius Richmond himself comments, "Knowledge alone does not create public policy, but its absence will ultimately limit our capacity to make good public policy" (Richmond & Kotelchuck, 1984, p. 207).

Recommendation #1: Achieve Definitional Clarity

Our review of research, and the subsequent need for meticulous clarification of what and whom each study addressed, confirmed the well-acknowledged and highly problematic lack of definitional clarity around a number of key terms and concepts. Definitional clarity is essential in that it will enable those in the ECE field to speak a "common language" and enable those outside the field to comprehend distinctions and nuances that must be understood to enable progress. Without common definitions, confusion will continue to reign, inhibiting integrated understanding, research, and policymaking. For that reason, and to end decades of debate and confusion, we recommend that a working group of early childhood experts be convened to create a common lexicon and establish systemwide definitions. In particular, this panel should proffer a set of working definitions regarding the following:

1. The umbrella term used to describe the field (we have used *early care and education*, but this is not uniformly accepted)
2. Terms used to describe subsections of the field (e.g., *sector, program*)
3. Terms and titles used to distinguish roles within the ECE workforce (e.g., *teacher, caregiver*)
4. Terms used to define various forms of professional development, training, and formal education

Such an effort must include representatives from major organizations, recognize the wide range of formal and informal services that characterize the ECE market, and build on the work of the Workgroup on Defining and Measuring Early Childhood Professional Development (2005). The effort should widely disseminate the definitions developed in order to promote consistent terminology in the field, in policies (at federal, state, and local levels), in research, and in data collection efforts.

Recommendation #2: Achieve Conceptual Clarity

Throughout this book, countless examples of conceptual challenges have been highlighted. In some cases, these challenges are exacerbated by a lack of definitions, as noted above. In other cases, challenges exist because there is limited understanding of the differentiated roles of the federal, state, and local governments with regard to the provision of ECE, or even of the diverse functions of program types within ECE. Further, there is limited understanding of the optimal relationship between the public and the private sectors, the way the ECE (non-)system functions as part of the human services industry, and the way both the ECE and human services industries function within the broader market economy. Without a broader conceptual framework, flavor-of-the-day practices, programs, and policies will proliferate independently and, we argue, make only piecemeal dents in improving ECE and its workforce. To create that framework, we recommend that the National Academy of Sciences, as the nation's most prestigious scientific body, establish a panel to achieve greater conceptual clarity around systemic ECE issues. Distinguished from the above working group (Recommendation #1), designed to address definitional clarity, this panel must strive to achieve conceptual clarity by discerning the following:

1. A workable delineation of responsibility among federal, state, and local governments regarding the delivery of ECE services
2. A workable relationship between the public and private sectors in the delivery of ECE services
3. Strategies to redress the market failure conditions that now characterize ECE and the ECE workforce (e.g., constraining private-sector resources to force public expenditures)
4. The evidentiary base to support the above proposals

Recommendation #3: Enhance Data and Research Capacities About ECE Policies and Programs

As the prior sections of this analysis have made abundantly clear, in the field of ECE, data, research, and research capacity are severely limited—and limiting. Data that are collected are sparse and inconsistent; they do not pertain to the field at large, but to subsegments of it; they are not collected with regular periodicity; they vary by state in accordance with state mandates; and, except for the National Household Education Survey (which is definitionally limited) and the Early Childhood Longitudinal Studies (which are cohort limited), national data that address the entire ECE workforce do not exist. In short, the contemporary research base is inadequate because it does not sufficiently include the following:

1. Consistent data across program types
2. Attention to child-related dependent variables (e.g., child outcomes)
3. Distinction among independent quality variables (e.g., program quality vs. classroom quality)
4. Agreement on the standards of evidence for ECE workforce studies
5. Analysis of the benefits of different forms of professional development for different individuals or programs
6. Information on the costs of professional development
7. Input from diverse scholars, using diverse research designs, from diverse disciplines, including political science, economics, history, and education
8. Mechanisms for collecting comprehensive baseline data that are representative of the total population

To build a first-rate national database, we recommend the establishment of a major, publicly funded National Institute of Early Care and Education (NIECE) akin to the National Institute for Child Health and Human Development. The NIECE would promote systematic inquiry and provide national data on critical issues pertaining to American ECE. Its work would have four foci: (1) the collection of ongoing surveys that provide descriptive data about the status of ECE; (2) the undertaking of research on the implementation and effectiveness of reforms; (3) the initiating, funding, and oversight of "ahead-of-the-curve" research that furthers the practice of ECE; and (4) econometric research related to the advancement of ECE.

In terms of ongoing surveys and descriptive research, the National Institute of Early Care and Education should initiate new and recurring (annual or biannual) survey data collections or enmesh ECE data with existing ongoing national data collections (e.g., the Schools and Staffing Survey). Data should be collected on all types of ECE settings and, apropos of this report, all ECE teachers, including FCC providers and FFN caregivers. These data should reflect the current status of the ECE field and should be widely popularized to policymakers and leaders. The data will serve as a bank to which researchers around the world would have access.

Second, NIECE should be home to teams of experts from diverse disciplines who would devote themselves to systemic study of key issues related to better understanding the implementation and effectiveness of workforce reforms related to ECE teacher quality, teacher education, professional development institutions, training, and credentials. The development of new instruments and measures to assess the nuances of teacher behavior and skills and the impacts of professional development on teacher performance and child outcomes is necessary. Relevant research questions include the following:

1. What should teachers of young children know and be able to do in order to carry out their work with efficacy?
2. How can we ensure that teachers are equipped to meet the needs of specific populations of children, including English Language Learners, infants and toddlers, and children with special needs?
3. What is the difference between classroom quality and teacher quality in ECE settings?
4. Are there particular thresholds of formal education or training that matter to child outcomes?
5. What is the comparative advantage of preservice versus inservice professional development for teacher performance?
6. What role do incentives play in changing ECE teachers' knowledge, skills, and behavior?

7. What are the independent effects of teachers' experience and compensation?
8. What kind of standards can ensure both content and pedagogical quality in technology-mediated learning?
9. What elements of the workforce environment directly impact teacher performance and child outcomes?
10. What impacts, if any, accrue from the mismatch between the diversity of America's child population and the predominantly White population of both ECE teachers and teacher educators?

Third, in terms of "ahead-of-the-curve" research, one arm of the NIECE should initiate seminal studies that would advance ECE practice and policies. Such work could include evaluations of innovative efforts, research and demonstration work, cross-national studies, and empirical work on issues pertinent to ECE. Analyses in this arena might include the following:

1. The pros and cons of unionizing the ECE workforce as it relates to teacher quality/child outcomes
2. The liabilities and advantages of collective management
3. The role of new governance structures in raising ECE program and teacher quality, as well as in improving child outcomes
4. The comparative impact of national monitoring on child outcomes

All of these recommendations—both those specific to the ECE workforce and those that impact the broader ECE system—will require substantially greater investment of both public and private resources in the ECE workforce. With such investments comes the need for greater accountability that ensures monies are being used efficiently and effectively. Indeed, the costs and funding of ECE and its workforce drive policy and policymakers. Except for a small number of studies, little attention has been paid to financing parameters of the ECE workforce. Moreover, as different kinds of analyses are modeled in other fields, their application to ECE should be fostered (Barnett & Kelley, 2006; Levin & McEwan, 2001). We recommend that NIECE allocate funds to support the development of a field-based capacity to handle diverse econometric analyses of ECE and its workforce. Such a compendium might include the following:

1. Cost–benefit analyses that measure the financial implications of interventions (i.e., the cost of turnover relative to the cost of interventions intended to reduce turnover)
2. Cost–effectiveness analyses that compare the costs and outcomes of alternative approaches

3. Cost–utility analyses that compare alternatives by examining their costs in comparison to their utility or satisfaction
4. Cost–feasibility analyses that investigate the cost of a single alternative so that funders can determine the effort's feasibility in light of available resources

STRATEGIES FOR ENHANCING POLITICAL AND PUBLIC WILL

To render comprehensive and long-lasting social change, political and public will must be durable, widespread, and dedicated to more than quick-fix, band-aid approaches to reform. Given that political and public will is the means for generating resources to carry out policies and programs, and given that reform of the ECE workforce requires systemic change, meaningful political and public will campaigns are absolutely necessary. As part of our overall social strategy, we suggest two recommendations that will contribute to expanding and strengthening the constituency for change on behalf of ECE teachers.

Recommendation #4: Take Promising Policies and Programs to Scale

As this book has noted, workforce improvement efforts are plentiful at the state, local, and program levels. These efforts represent emergent political and public will, and they provide solid examples of effective approaches to improving ECE teachers' professional development, compensation, and working conditions. Moreover, in developing these efforts, implementation capacity has grown, as has a cadre of workforce pioneers whose expertise can inform expanded workforce reform efforts. The question at hand is how to go about taking these noteworthy efforts and expanding them, bringing them to a large enough scale to improve the ECE teaching workforce as a whole.

In examining social change strategies, small efforts commonly are expanded at the state level. This makes sense in ECE on two counts. First, because states are so diverse in their population and approaches to workforce enhancement, they are natural laboratories of planned variation. Second, most ECE programs have some relationship to the state, either through program regulations, child-based subsidies, or grant funding. Using the state as the unit of change, therefore, makes sense. Thus, the states, their personnel, and their workforce programs are a potent lever for workforce advancements. We recommend the establishment of mechanisms that permit states to take policies or programs that have been delimited—by geography, market sector, or program type—and expand them to all ECE teachers.

One way to incentivize the establishment of such mechanisms is through the development of major demonstration efforts in five states. The purpose of the demonstration grants would be to build upon existing programs, expanding them to become more systemic and linking them to ambitious reforms at the national level. As will be explicated in detail below (see Recommendations #6 and #7), we propose radical changes to how the ECE workforce is credentialed, prepared, and compensated. Demonstration grants would enable states to fuse their ongoing work with newly proposed national credentialing and competency assessment efforts. States interested in pioneering the linkage between the recommendations herein and their existing or planned efforts would be selected on a competitive basis for their diversity of approach and their proven capacity and competence for systemic reform. One evidentiary base for dedication to systemic reform should include plans to either develop or expand a statewide quality rating system that provides the following:

1. Inclusion of all ECE programs
2. Multiple, achievable levels of quality that clearly articulate professional development ladders, compensation ladders, and work environment standards
3. Financial incentives to support program improvement
4. Multiple strategies to mobilize political and public awareness
5. Evaluation of the impact on teachers and children

Each state would receive 5-year funding based on the submission of a proposal that would delineate the goals, challenges, timelines, and parties involved in reforming the ECE teaching workforce. By definition, states submitting proposals would accept the national recommendations presented in this book and would work to implement them in conjunction with state-initiated workforce initiatives.

Such a demonstration effort would be large—$2 million of federal funds distributed annually to each of five states for 5 years. The demonstration effort would be accompanied by formative, process, and summative evaluations conducted by the National Institute for Early Care and Education (see Recommendation #3 above). States involved in the demonstration effort would have the opportunity to share their work— accomplishments and challenges —with one another, solicit technical assistance, and disseminate their work broadly. The five efforts will serve as learning laboratories for the rest of the states, using a turnkey or mentoring model that would foster the implementation of these approaches in additional states throughout the nation.

Recommendation #5: Build ECE Political and Public Will for the Development of an ECE System

The ECE field has been quite successful in using the media to advance overall public understanding of the importance of the early years and the contributions that high-quality ECE makes to children's development during those years. Unfortunately, far less effort has been mobilized to advance the importance of ECE teachers or an ECE system. A fresh media approach should be launched to publicize the importance of developing an ECE system with a highly qualified workforce: We recommend that a media campaign be launched in which a cadre of high-profile individuals (e.g., movie stars, corporate executives, policymakers), working in conjunction with the private sector, vocally and visibly emphasize and support ECE workforce issues. The campaign would pursue press and broadcast media strategies, with the goal of generating public understanding of the crucial role played by ECE teachers and the political and public support needed to undertake comprehensive efforts to improve their training, certification, and compensation. Such an effort would use techniques that have proven successful in other social reform efforts and would be integrated into reform efforts as an ongoing and sustained component.

STRATEGIES THAT DIRECTLY IMPACT THE ECE TEACHING WORKFORCE

The above recommendations relating to the knowledge base and to political and public will are central to the ultimate reform and improvement of the ECE workforce; without them, comprehensive and sustainable reform is not possible. They all, however, have only indirect impact on ECE teachers. To truly improve the day-to-day experiences and effectiveness of ECE teachers, there must be bold recommendations targeted directly to ECE teachers' professional development, compensation, and working conditions. The following three recommendations do just that.

Recommendation #6: Systematize All ECE Lead Teacher Entry Qualifications to a Common High-Quality Standard by Creating a National Credential and National Competency Assessment

Throughout this book, we have noted repeatedly both the importance of a quality teaching workforce to positive child outcomes and the legion of problems caused by highly inconsistent, low, or even nonexistent entry requirements for ECE teachers. To both elevate and equalize entry requirements for ECE teachers across programs and across states, we recommend instituting a National Credential that all lead teachers in all ECE settings would need to possess in order to have primary responsibility for a group of young children. This National Credential would be awarded only after satisfactory performance on a new National Competency Assessment. Composed of a written test of knowledge and observation of teachers' instructional ability, the National Competency Assessment would measure whether lead teachers had the requisite disposition, knowledge, skills, and abilities to work effectively with young children and their families. Current ECE lead teachers would be "grandfathered," but all individuals entering lead teacher roles would be required to possess the National Credential based on their successful completion of the National Competency Assessment.

The idea of a National Credential and a National Competency Assessment is not new. Indeed, ECE can look to other fields, as well as to its own history, for a successful array of such efforts. In many fields that serve the public (e.g., nursing, social work, K–12 teaching, and cosmetology), a credential that certifies qualification to practice in the field is required. Credentials serve many functions; they identify a discrete body of knowledge, establish a set of specified skills, and certify that an individual is qualified to carry out expected roles and responsibilities according to rigorous standards. In so doing, credentials bring other benefits. For the credentialed individual, they often are accompanied by increased recognition, increased commitment to the field, and increased compensation. The public benefits, as well, in that credentials provide a safeguard, signaling a level of competence or achievement by the individual.

Recognizing the need for, and importance of, credentialing in early care and education, the Child Development Associate (CDA) credential was established in 1971 to certify the competence of beginner-level ECE teachers. Serving the field well over time, the CDA can function as a platform for credentialing more seasoned or lead teachers who develop, implement, and monitor instructional programs for young children. The existence of the CDA, as well as credentials from other fields, benefit ECE because they form a base from which to understand the elements that need to be included in, and the gains to be achieved from, credentialing efforts. Most frequently, such efforts entail competency assessments in two parts: (1) a standardized written test, and (2) a demonstration of knowledge and skills. For the National Credential for ECE lead teachers, the written test would assess candidates' knowledge of child development and early childhood education, the pedagogical and ethical canons of the field, and the importance of working with diverse cultures, families, and communities. Complementing the test, direct observations of the candidates would provide firsthand

evidence of their skills in classroom management and in facilitating positive learning environments for all children. While challenging to formu-
late, the benefits of such a credential are huge, particularly given the
problems of state and program inconsistency made apparent in this volume. Specifically, the existence of a National Credential and a National
Competency Assessment would: (1) establish the knowledge and behaviors expected of all lead teachers responsible for working with young children, irrespective of state or delivery setting; (2) communicate clearly to
parents and the public that working with groups of young children requires
specialized knowledge and expertise; (3) safeguard a level of competence
and quality for America's young children; and (4) pave the pathway for
increased compensation.

Similar to the nursing profession, which administers its competency
credential to individuals with an AA or BA degree, the prerequisite to
take the ECE National Competency Assessment would be the completion of an AA or BA degree; upon successful completion of the National
Competency Assessment, an individual with either formal degree would
be credentialed as a lead teacher. These requirements would apply to lead
teachers in centers and family child care homes, in for-profit and nonprofit
settings, and in high- and low-ECE-spending states. This requirement
would move the field forward in terms of raising the level of education
expected of lead teachers, while also anchoring teacher qualifications in
demonstrated competence.

Much like in the nursing field, while the ECE competency assessment
would be national in scope and the National Credential would be awarded
nationally, we recommend that each state establish an ECE Teacher Licensing Board to award licenses. Here, we distinguish between the National
Credential, which would be competency-based and uniform across the states,
and licensure, which would be state-based and state-administered. It is expected that no state would award a lead teacher license to an individual
who did not have the National Credential, thereby setting an equitable
baseline of teacher competency that spans all programs and states across
the country.

The bulk of this recommendation is geared toward lead teachers. To
address the qualifications of those who do not have primary responsibility for children in ECE programs, we recommend that every assistant-level
teacher be required to hold a minimum of a Child Development Associate
credential. While lead and assistant teachers would be required to demonstrate a specific (though different) level of competence in the field, each
would have different roles and responsibilities, with lead teachers super-
vising assistant teachers.

This recommendation is tied closely to our next ECE teaching workforce-specific recommendation, which addresses not only the mechanisms by which this competency assessment would be developed and administered, but also the professional development and education systems that prepare teachers to pass the assessment.

Recommendation #7: Foster Highly Effective and Consistent ECE Teacher Preparation and Licensure by Creating a National ECE Teacher Education Compact

Both to support and to implement a National Credential for ECE teachers, based on successfully passing a National Competency Assessment (Recommendation #6), and to raise the quality of institutions that provide training and education to potential and current ECE teachers, we recommend creating a National ECE Teacher Education Compact. The purposes of the Compact would be to (1) set the standards for the National Competency Assessment, including both the test of knowledge and the performance demonstration; (2) administer the National Competency Assessment, including the credentialing of teachers who pass the assessment; and (3) ensure that the quality standards established by existing organizations for informal professional development, vocational-technical programs, and 2- and 4-year institutions of higher education are aligned with one another and with the National Competency Assessment.

First, the Compact must set the standards for the National Competency Assessment, develop the written test and observational tool, administer the assessment system to all potential lead teachers who enter ECE, and credential those who pass the National Competency Assessment. In accordance with the increasingly diverse population in the United States, the standards of competency in ECE must extend beyond teachers' ability to establish and maintain a safe and healthy learning environment, and focus on improving teachers' ability to use effective pedagogical strategies that encourage children to acquire age-appropriate skills, knowledge, and behaviors. The National Competency Assessment should set standards related to teachers' ability to engage and support families, exhibit cultural competency, observe and assess young children, teach English Language Learners, and work with infants and toddlers, children with special needs, mixed-age groups, and large groups of children.

Second, as administrator of the National Competency Assessment, the Compact must ensure that the assessment is conducted with fidelity, quality, and equity. Moreover, the Compact must grant credentials to those ECE teachers who pass the assessment. This credential will be recognized nationally as evidence of a teacher's competence to be a lead ECE teacher. As noted in Recommendation #6, we hope that each state will establish an ECE Teacher Licensing Board that will require all individuals who wish to become lead ECE teachers to possess the National Credential before being granted a license to teach in any program.

To implement the third function—ensuring alignment of quality standards for providers of training and institutions of higher education—the Compact must collaborate closely with existing initiatives led by the National Association for the Education of Young Children (NAEYC), the National Council for Accreditation of Teacher Education (NCATE), and ACCESS (an association of ECE teacher educators in 2-year colleges), which, together, accredit 2-year, 4-year, and vocational-technical programs. In addition, the Compact would build upon the effort of the National Association of Child Care Resource and Referral Agencies (NACCRRA) to set standards of quality for more informal professional development offerings and providers.

To do this, the Compact would convene representatives from NAEYC, NCATE, ACCESS, and NACCRRA to review and, where necessary, revise their respective accreditation standards, to ensure that the content of education and training reflects the content and expectations embedded in the National Teacher Competency Assessment. The standards should ensure that institutions recruit and retain teacher educators and trainers in adequate numbers and with high levels of both theoretical knowledge and practical experience. In addition, the accreditation standards should ensure that teacher education and training provided by all institutions reflect best practices in adult learning and are equitably accessible to both center- and home-based teachers. Moreover, to be accredited, each institution must ensure that its teachers in training receive courses specifically focused on working with diverse children and families, individualized professional development (e.g., mentoring, coaching), and a means to reflect on their own beliefs. In addition, the Compact, in partnership with the above-named national organizations involved in ECE teachers' professional development, would develop a series of supports—and, ultimately, consequences—for those institutions and professional development providers that fail to achieve quality standards.

The creation of such a Compact would radically change the relationship among government, institutions of higher education, and organizations and individuals that provide professional development to ECE teachers. Most notably, this recommendation would establish a quality framework applicable to the full range of programs that provide ECE teachers' formal education and professional development, thereby determining which institutions of higher education and providers of professional development deliver the highest quality teacher training functions. In addition, this recommendation would provide a means for improving and, if necessary, sanctioning those institutions and programs that continually fail to meet quality performance standards.

The establishment of a national compact to not only set standards for a National Competency Assessment that credentials teachers, but also ensure alignment of accreditation standards for the institutions that provide training and education to teachers, is not a new idea. England created the Teacher Training Agency in 1994 to reform and improve teacher quality in its system of primary and secondary education (Ellis, 2006). International exemplars may help guide the creation of an American Compact.

Recommendation #8: Increase ECE Teachers' Compensation and Benefits

The last two recommendations specifically address the qualifications of teachers and the quality of formal education and training they receive. These efforts, though, will not be sustainable and will not encourage dedication to the ECE field without a third recommendation: The establishment of funding mechanisms that increase ECE teachers' compensation and comprehensive benefits. Fair wages are only one component of a compensation package that will attract and retain bright, ambitious, and nurturing adults into the ECE field. Wages must be accompanied by financial assistance that encourages adults not only to achieve a level of training and education adequate to pass the National Competency Assessment, but also to pursue ongoing training that keeps their skills and knowledge up-to-date and encourages a lifetime of learning. A comprehensive benefits package, including health insurance and retirement savings, is also necessary to raise the occupation of ECE teaching to a level commensurate with other professions.

To boost ECE teachers' compensation to parity with that of K–12 teachers, and to extend wage enhancement efforts beyond local communities and subsections of the field, both federal and state strategies are necessary. At the federal level, to encourage programs to pay ECE teachers higher wages and to encourage teachers who are currently employed in programs (and, therefore, not required to pass the National Competency Assessment) to become licensed, we propose that ECE programs that meet quality criteria be awarded "compensation grants." These grants would increase teachers' earnings at center- and home-based programs in which all lead teachers have passed the National Competency Assessment and all assistant teachers hold a CDA. The grants must be given only to programs that link wage enhancement with other policies that guarantee higher quality early care and education. These linkages could include (but not be limited to) efforts to establish career ladders that recognize and reward participation in ongoing professional development, to provide ongoing training to program administrators, to serve children in high-needs communities, or to work with specific populations of children (e.g., English Language Learners, infants and toddlers, children with special needs).

These grants should be paid from a comprehensive federal fund comprising both public sources (e.g., Child Care Development Fund, Title I, Head Start) and private sources (e.g., endowment funds established by national foundations). While the federal compensation grants can contribute substantially to programs' ability to provide fair compensation and benefits to ECE teachers, states also must increase their commitment to, and investment in, ECE teacher compensation.

Because each state's context, economy, population, and level and nature of public investments vary greatly, each state must establish an ongoing mechanism to support ECE teachers, much as they do now through their K–12 funding formulas. We offer three potential state-level mechanisms to generate the revenue needed to bolster ECE teacher compensation. First, states could incorporate young children into their K–12 funding formula, thereby explicitly putting ECE on a par with K–12 and ECE teachers on a par with teachers of older children. Second, states could increase and earmark individual and corporate income taxes, thereby distributing the tax burden between individuals and businesses, both of which would benefit directly from the expansion of higher quality ECE programs. This would provide financial incentives for all families at all income levels to choose higher quality early care and education. Third, states could expand and earmark payroll taxes, also distributing the burden equally between families and business, but taxing only earned income.

ECE teachers must be able to afford the education and training required to successfully pass the National Competency Assessment. To do this, a public system of financial assistance must be developed to support individuals pursuing education and training that prepare them to pass the assessment. This financial assistance should be a combination of loans and scholarships provided on a sliding-fee scale according to each individual's ability to pay. In these respects, the financial assistance in higher education is a model that should be examined and adapted to meet the needs of the ECE workforce. Further, a federal loan forgiveness program should be reinstituted whereby a percentage of a borrower's loan is forgiven for each consecutive year the teacher works in an ECE program. Any teacher who works for 3 consecutive years after graduation should have 100% of the loan forgiven.

To attract and retain talented ECE teachers, it is important that they be offered adequate pensions. Today, colleges and universities offer some of the best retirement plans in the nation; programs and institutions that nurture and educate the nation's youngest children deserve no less. TIAA-CREF, one of the world's largest retirement systems, serves more than 15,000 colleges, universities, schools, research centers, medical organizations, and other nonprofit institutions throughout the United States. Through the Compact recommended above, all ECE teachers who have passed the National Competency Assessment should be eligible to participate in a TIAA-CREF group retirement annuity contract. Both the employee and the employer would invest in the fund through a variety of investment and income options, providing flexibility for each ECE teacher to determine best how to plan for the future.

Finally, it is crucial that ECE teachers have adequate and reliable health insurance. To incentivize employer-sponsored health insurance, the Compact should establish, via a contract with an independent insurance company (or companies), an insurance program into which community-based and home-based ECE programs can opt, thereby creating an economy of scale similar to those already present in Military Child Care and public school-based ECE. Monthly premiums would be paid by a combination of contributions from the employer, the government, and the employee. Each participating program would be required to contribute a specified amount each month for each employee, which would be matched by the government. Only after the employer and the government had contributed matching amounts, would costs be passed on to employees. In addition to employer-sponsored insurance packages, similar to the insurance services provided by the American Association of Retired Persons (AARP), individual ECE teachers could purchase supplemental insurance through the same entity.

While comprehensive wage and benefits reform seems ambitious, it is not without precedent. In 2005, a coalition of nonprofit advocacy organizations developed federal legislation that would improve the quality of ECE by helping to end the high turnover of ECE teachers through the improvement of their compensation. The FOCUS (Focus on Committed and Underpaid Staff for Children's Sake) Act, sponsored by Senator Christopher Dodd and Representative George Miller, would establish a Child Care Provider Scholarship Program for ECE teachers pursuing higher education in fields related to early childhood development. It also would create a Child Care Provider Development and Retention Grant Program to reward and encourage qualified teachers with grants and stipends. Finally, the FOCUS bill would establish a Child Care Provider Health Benefits Coverage Program to make health coverage accessible to ECE teachers through subsidized health plans (Legal Momentum, 2006). Although this legislation is still only a policy proposal, it represents a promising example of how comprehensive wage and benefits reform can be undertaken on behalf of ECE teachers.

CONCLUSION

We conclude this book with two overarching points. First, the ECE workforce is a fulcrum in terms of its function; no one can deny the central role the ECE workforce plays for children, families, and the economy. Second, we hope this book will serve as a fulcrum in time—a turning point for the ECE workforce; after reading this volume, no one can deny the urgency of the moment or the possibilities at hand. The ECE workforce is in a precarious state, caught in the balance between creating a new, equitable, and systemic approach to professional development, and languishing even more deeply into a quality crisis. The data presented herein give evidence of promising models and approaches that could propel the former and prevent the latter. We conclude with appreciation for what has been accomplished and, based on this, with fervent optimism that what can and should be done, will be achieved. In this book, with Julius Richmond's mission in mind, we have tried to provide a means to accomplish all three of his conditions for revolutionary social change. We have done so in order to tip the balance, permanently altering the vulnerability and precariousness of the ECE teachers at the fulcrum.

References

AACTE Focus Council on Early Childhood Education. (2004). *The early childhood challenge: Preparing high-quality teachers for a changing society*. Washington, DC: American Association of Colleges for Teachers of Education.

Ackerman, D. J. (2006, April). *"The learning never stops": Lessons from military child development centers for teacher professional development*. Paper presented at the annual meeting of the American Educational Research Association, San Francisco.

Adams, D., Bierbrauer, J., Edie, D., Riley, D., & Roach, M. (2003). *T.E.A.C.H. Early Childhood® Wisconsin evaluation report (August 1999–June 2003)*. Madison: Wisconsin Child Care Research Partnership, University of Wisconsin— Extension.

Adema, W. (2001). *Net social expenditure* (2nd ed.) (Labor Market and Social Policy Occasional Papers, No. 52). Paris: OECD.

Ball, D. L., & Cohen, D. K. (1996). Reform by the book: What is—or might be— the role of curriculum materials in teacher learning and instructional reform? *Educational Researcher, 25*(9), 6–8.

Barnett, W. S. (2003a). *Better teachers, better preschools: Student achievement linked to teacher qualifications* (Preschool Policy Matters, Issue 2). New Brunswick, NJ: National Institute for Early Education Research.

Barnett, W. S. (2003b). *Low wages = low quality: Solving the real preschool teacher crisis* (Preschool Policy Matters, Issue 3). New Brunswick, NJ: National Institute for Early Education Research.

Barnett, W. S., Hustedt, J. T., Hawkinson, L. H., & Robin, K. B. (2006). *The state of preschool 2006: State preschool yearbook*. New Brunswick, NJ: National Institute for Early Education Research.

Barnett, W. S., & Kelley, P. J. (2006). A framework for cost-benefit analysis of professional development in early care and education. In M. Zaslow & I. Martinez-Beck (Eds.), *Critical issues in early childhood professional development* (pp. 313–338). Baltimore: Paul H. Brookes.

Bellm, D., Burton, A., Whitebook, M., Broatch, L., & Young, M. (2002). *Inside the pre-K classroom: A study of staffing and stability in state-funded prekindergarten programs*. Washington, DC: Center for the Child Care Workforce.

Berk, L. E. (1985). Relationship of caregiver education to child-oriented attitudes, job satisfaction, and behaviors toward children. *Child Care Quarterly, 14*(2), 103–129.

Blase, J. (1999). Principals' instructional leadership and teacher development: Teachers' perspectives. *Educational Administration Quarterly, 35*(33), 349–378.

Blau, D. M. (2000). The production of quality in child-care centers: Another look. *Applied Developmental Science, 4*(3), 136–148.

Boots, S. W. (2006). *Preparing quality teachers for PK–3: FCD meeting summary.* New York: Foundation for Child Development.

Bowman, B. T., Donovan, M. S., & Burns, M. S. (Eds.). (2001). *Eager to learn: Educating our preschoolers.* Washington, DC: National Academy Press.

Boyd, B. J., & Schneider, N. I. (1997). Perceptions of the work environment and burnout in Canadian child care providers. *Journal of Research in Childhood Education, 11,* 171–180.

Boyd, B. J., & Wandschneider, M. R. (2004). *Washington State Child Care Career and Wage Ladder Pilot Project: Phase 2 final evaluation report.* Pullman: Washington State University, Department of Human Development.

Brandon, R. N. (2005). *Enhancing family friend and neighbor caregiving quality: The research case for public engagement.* Seattle: University of Washington, Human Services Policy Center.

Brandon, R. N., Kagan, S. L., & Joesch, J. M. (2000). *Design choices: Universal financing for early care and education.* Seattle: University of Washington, Human Services Policy Center.

Brandon, R. N., Maher, E. J., Joesch, J. M., & Doyle, S. (2002). *Understanding family, friend, and neighbor care in Washington State: Developing appropriate training and support.* Seattle: University of Washington, Human Services Policy Center.

Bredekamp, S., & Copple, C. (1997). *Developmentally appropriate practice in early childhood programs.* Washington, DC: National Association for the Education of Young Children.

Bright from the Start. (2006). *2006–2007 school year pre-K providers operating guidelines.* Atlanta: Georgia Department of Early Care and Learning.

Brooks, F. P. (2003). What differences unionizing teachers might make on child care in the USA: Results from an exploratory study. *Child and Youth Care Forum, 32*(1), 3–22.

Brooks, F. P. (2005). New turf for organizing: Family child care providers. *Labor Studies Journal, 29*(4), 45–64.

Brown, J. G., & Hallam, R. (2004). A comprehensive report of child care providers' perceptions of a statewide early care and education initiative. *Child and Youth Care Forum, 33*(1), 19–31.

Brown, M. (2002). Project PRIMER at South Carolina State University [Electronic version]. *Communique: Head Start Higher Education Partnerships, 1*(1). Retrieved June 25, 2006, from http://www.acf.hhs.gov/programs/hsb/publications/communiqueMay02.htm#project

Brown-Lyons, M., Robertson, A., & Layzer, J. (2001). *Kith and kin—Informal child care: Highlights from recent research.* New York: Columbia University, National Center for Children in Poverty.

Bruner, C. (with Wright, M. S., Gebhard, B., & Hibbard, S.). (2004). *Building an early learning system: The ABC's of planning and governance structures* (Resource Brief). Des Moines, IA: State Early Childhood Policy Technical Assistance Network and the Build Initiative.

Burchinal, M., Cryer, D., Clifford, R. M., & Howes, C. (2002). Caregiver training and classroom quality in child care centers. *Applied Developmental Science, 6*(1), 2–11.

Burchinal, M., Howes, C., & Kontos, S. (2002). Structural predictors of child care quality in child care homes. *Early Childhood Research Quarterly, 17*(1), 87–105.

Bureau of Labor Statistics. (2004, May 10). *Characteristics of minimum wage workers: 2003.* Retrieved January 8, 2007, from http://www.bls.gov/cps/minwage2003.htm

Bureau of Labor Statistics. (2005). *Occupational outlook handbook, 2006–07 edition, child care workers.* Retrieved February 13, 2006, from http://www.bls.gov/oco/ocos170.htm

Bureau of Labor Statistics. (2006a). *May 2005 national occupational employment and wage estimates.* Retrieved November 6, 2006, from http://www.bls.gov/oes/current/oes_nat.htm

Bureau of Labor Statistics. (2006b). *Occupational outlook handbook, 2006–07 edition, Teachers—Preschool, kindergarten, elementary, middle, and secondary.* Retrieved June 5, 2006, from http://www.bls.gov/oco/ocos069.htm

Burton, A., Whitebook, M., Young, M., Bellm, D., Wayne, C., & Brandon, R. N. (2002). *Estimating the size and components of the U.S. child care workforce and caregiving population: Key findings from the child care workforce estimate* (Preliminary Report). Washington, DC: Center for the Child Care Workforce and Human Services Policy Center.

California Early Childhood Mentor Program. (n.d.). *Improving care.* Retrieved February 2, 2006, from http://www.ecementor.org/Care.htm

California Institute on Human Services and Sonoma State University. (n.d.). *Hilton/Early Head Start training program.* Retrieved June 22, 2006, from http://specialquest.org/sq.htm

Campbell, N. D., Applebaum, J. C., Martinson, K., & Martin, E. (2000). *Be all that we can be: Lessons from the military for improving our nation's child care system.* Washington, DC: National Women's Law Center.

Caspary, K., Gilman, E., & Hamilton, M. (2002). *Alameda Child Development Corps: Year 1 qualitative implementation study.* Berkeley: Policy Analysis for California Education.

Center for Family Policy and Research. (2005). *Project REACH* (Rural EArly CHildhood Educational Institute). Retrieved August 10, 2006, from http://www.missouri.edu/~cfprwww/reach.html

Center for the Child Care Workforce. (2006a). *Low salaries for staff, high costs to children.* Washington, DC: Author.

Center for the Child Care Workforce. (2006b). Washington State advocates win $1 million for the career and wage ladder [Electronic version]. *Rights, Raises, Respect: News and Issues for the Early Care and Education Workforce: A Monthly Electronic Newsletter.* Retrieved January 22, 2007, from http://www.ccw.org/pubs/Newsletter0603.pdf

Center on the Social and Emotional Foundations for Early Learning. (n.d.). *About us.* Retrieved July 15, 2006, from http://csefel.uiuc.edu/

Child Care Bureau. (2004a). *Fiscal year 2004 federal child care appropriations.* Retrieved February 17, 2006, from http://www.acf.hhs.gov/programs/ccb/policy1/misc/approp04.htm

Child Care Bureau. (2004b, October 13). *From blueprint to reality: Early learning guidelines implementation.* Paper presented at the Good Start, Grow Smart: State Early Learning Guidelines Roundtable, Washington, DC.

Child Care Bureau. (2006). *Overview of the Child Care and Development Fund* (fiscal years 2006–2007). Retrieved May 4, 2007, from http://www.acf.hhs.gov/programs/ccb/ccdf/ccdf06–07desc.htm

Child Care Services Association. (2003). *Working in child care in North Carolina: The North Carolina child care workforce survey.* Chapel Hill: Author.

Child Care Services Association. (2004). *Health insurance program.* Retrieved January 20, 2007, from http://www.childcareservices.org/ps/health_ins.html

Child Care Services Association. (2005a). *Child Care WAGE$® project statewide final report: July 2004–June 2005.* Chapel Hill, NC: Author.

Child Care Services Association. (2005b). *T.E.A.C.H. Early Childhood® annual report, July 1, 2004–June 30, 2005.* Chapel Hill, NC: Author.

Child Care Services Association. (2005c). *T.E.A.C.H. Early Childhood® project.* Retrieved January 20, 2006, from http://www.childcareservices.org/teach/project.html

Child Care Services Association. (2005d). *T.E.A.C.H. Early Childhood® state contacts.* Retrieved January 20, 2006, from http://www.childcareservices.org/teach/states.htm

City and County of San Francisco Department of Human Services. (2004). *Wages Plus, Wages Plus Quality+, and Wages+ Family Child Care.* San Francisco: Author.

Clarke-Stewart, K. A., Vandell, D. L., Burchinal, M., O'Brien, M., & McCartney, K. (2002). Do regulable features of child-care homes affect children's development? *Early Childhood Research Quarterly, 17*(1), 52–86.

Coffman, J., & Lopez, M. E. (2003). *Raising preschool teacher qualifications.* Washington, DC: Trust for Early Education and the Harvard Family Research Project.

College Invest. (n.d.). *Early childhood development professional loan repayment program.* Retrieved March 7, 2006, from http://www.collegeinvest.org/How%20Our%20Loans%20Help/EarlyChild.htm

Connecticut Charts-A-Course. (2005). *Connecticut Charts-A-Course year end report 2004–2005.* New Haven: Author.

Consumer Education Quality Assurance Program. (2002). *Criteria for best practices in the delivery of consumer education and referral.* Arlington, VA: National Association of Child Care Resource and Referral Agencies.

Cornille, T. A., Mullis, R. L., Mullis, A. K., & Shriner, M. (2006). An examination of childcare teachers in for-profit and non-profit childcare centers. *Early Child Development and Care, 176*(6), 631–641.

Cost, Quality, and Child Outcomes Study Team. (1995). *Cost, quality, and child outcomes in child care centers.* Denver: University of Colorado, Economics Department.

Crandall, S. R. (2004). Promoting employer practices that increase retention and advancement [Electronic version]. *Welfare Information Network: Issue Notes, 8.* Retrieved February 15, 2007, from http://www.financeproject.org/Publications/promotingemployerpracticesIN.htm

de Kruif, R. E. L., McWilliam, R. A., Ridley, S. M., & Wakely, M. B. (2000). Classification of teachers' interaction behaviors in early childhood classrooms. *Early Childhood Research Quarterly, 15*(2), 247–268.

De Vita, C. J., & Montilla, M. D. (2003). *Improving child care quality: A comparison of military and civilian approaches* (Policy Brief: Charting Civil Society). Washington, DC: Urban Institute.

Department of Defense. (n.d.). *MilitaryHOMEFRONT: Military child care home.* Retrieved July 21, 2006, from http://www.militaryhomefront.dod.mil/portal/page/itc/MHF/MHF_HOME_1?section_id=20.60.500.390.0.0.0.0.0

Department of Health and Human Services. (2001, February 13). *Annual update of the HHS poverty guidelines.* Retrieved January 8, 2007, from http://aspe.hhs.gov/poverty/01fedreg.htm

Dickinson, D. K., & Brady, J. P. (2006). Toward effective support for language and literacy through professional development. In M. Zaslow & I. Martinez-Beck (Eds.), *Critical issues in early childhood professional development* (pp. 141–170). Baltimore: Paul H. Brookes.

Doherty, G., & Forer, B. (2002). *Unionization and quality in early childhood programs.* Ottawa, Canada: Canadian Union of Public Employees.

Donahue, E. H., & Campbell, N. D. (2002). *Making care less taxing: Improving state child and dependent care tax provisions.* Washington, DC: National Women's Law Center.

Drake, P. J., Unti, L., Greenspoon, B., & Fawcett, L. K. (2004). *First 5 California informal child caregiver support project focus groups and interviews report: Executive summary.* Scotts Valley: First 5 California Children and Families Commission and ETR Associates.

Early, D. M., Barbarin, O., Bryant, D., Burchinal, M. R., Chang, F., Clifford, R. M., et al. (2005). *Pre-kindergarten in eleven states: NCEDL's multi-state study of pre-kindergarten & Study of state-wide early education programs (SWEEP), preliminary descriptive report.* Chapel Hill: University of North Carolina.

Early, D. M., Bryant, D. M., Pianta, R. C., Clifford, R. M., Burchinal, M. R., Ritchie, S., et al. (2006). Are teachers' education, major, and credentials related to classroom quality and children's academic gains in pre-kindergarten? *Early Childhood Research Quarterly, 21*(2), 174–195.

Early, D. M., & Winton, P. J. (2001). Preparing the workforce: Early childhood teacher preparation at 2- and 4-year institutions of higher education. *Early Childhood Research Quarterly, 16*(3), 285–306.

Ellis, A. (2006). *Improving teacher training provision in England: 1990–2005.* London: PA Consulting Group.

Epstein, A. S. (1999). Pathways to quality in Head Start, public school, and private nonprofit early childhood programs. *Journal of Research in Early Childhood Education, 13*(2), 101–119.

Evans, G. D., Bryant, N. E., Owens, J. S., & Koukos, K. (2004). Ethnic differences in burnout, coping, and intervention acceptability among childcare professionals. *Child and Youth Care Forum, 33*(5), 349–371.

Ewan, D., & Matthews, H. (2006). *The potential of Title I for high-quality preschool* [PowerPoint]. Washington, DC: Center for Law and Social Policy.

Federal Student Aid. (2002). *Child care provider loan forgiveness program.* Retrieved February 17, 2006, from http://studentaid.ed.gov/PORTALSWebApp/students/english/childcare.jsp?tab=repaying

Feeney, S., & Freemen, N. K. (1999). *Ethics and the early childhood educator: Using the NAEYC Code.* Washington, DC: National Association for the Education of Young Children.

Fein, G. G. (1994). Preparing tomorrow's inventors. In S. G. Goffin & D. E. Day (Eds.), *New perspectives in early childhood teacher education: Bringing practitioners into the debate* (pp. 135–145). New York: Teachers College Press.

Fiene, R. (2002). Improving child care quality through an infant caregiver mentoring project. *Child and Youth Care Forum, 31*(2), 79–87.

First 5 California. (2006). *First 5 California: Comprehensive Approaches to Raising Educational Standards (CARES) for the early learning workforce county progress report summary 2004–2005 data.* Retrieved April 28, 2007, from http://www.edgateway.net/cs/cares/print/docs/cares/at_a_glance.html

Folbre, N. (2006). Demanding quality: Worker/Consumer coalitions and "high road" strategies in the care sector. *Politics & Society, 34*(1), 1–21.

Frank Porter Graham Child Development Institute. (2006). *Quality interventions for early care and education: Overview.* Retrieved February 22, 2006, from http://www.fpg.unc.edu/~quince/index.cfm

Gable, S., & Halliburton, A. (2003). Barriers to child care providers' professional development. *Child and Youth Care Forum, 32*(3), 175–193.

Gallagher, J. J., Clifford, R. M., & Maxwell, K. (2004). Getting from here to there: To an ideal early preschool system [Electronic version]. *Early Childhood Research and Practice, 6.* Retrieved January 22, 2007, from http://ecrp.uiuc.edu/v6n1/clifford.html

Garcia, E. E. (2001). *Hispanic education in the United States: Raices y alas.* Lanham, MD: Rowman & Littlefield.

Garcia, E. E., Jensen, B., & Cuellar, D. (2006). Early academic achievement of Hispanics in the United States: Implications for teacher preparation. *The New Educator, 2,* 123–147.

Ghazvini, A., & Mullis, R. L. (2002). Center-based care for young children: Examining predictors of quality. *Journal of Genetic Psychology, 163*(1), 112–125.

Gilliam, W. S., & Marchesseault, C. M. (2005). *From capitols to classrooms, policies to practice: State-funded prekindergarten at the classroom level: Part 1. Who's teaching our youngest students? Teacher education and training, experience, compensation and benefits, and assistant teachers.* New Haven, CT: Yale University, Yale Child Study Center.

Golin, S. C., Mitchell, A., & Gault, B. (2004). *The price of schools readiness: A tool for estimating the cost of universal preschool in the states.* Washington, DC: Institute for Women's Policy Research.

Granger, R. C., & Marx, E. (1990). The policy implications of compensation and working conditions in three publicly funded early childhood systems. *Early Childhood Research Quarterly, 5*(2), 181–198.

Grieshaber, S. (2001). Advocacy and early childhood educators: Identity and cultural conflicts. In S. Grieshaber & G. S. Cannella (Eds.), *Embracing identities in early childhood education: Diversity and possibilities* (pp. 60–72). New York: Teachers College Press.

Hacker, J. (2003). *The divided welfare state: The battle over public and private social benefits in the United States*. Cambridge: Cambridge University Press.

Hall, P., & Soskice, D. (Eds.). (2001). *Varieties of capitalism: The institutional foundations of comparative advantage*. New York: Oxford University Press.

Hamm, K. (2006). *More than meets the eye: Head Start programs, participants, families, and staff in 2005* (Head Start Series, Brief No. 8). Washington, DC: Center for Law and Social Policy.

Hamm, K., Gault, B., & Jones-DeWeever, A. (2005). *In our own backyards: Local and state strategies to improve the quality of family child care*. Washington, DC: Institute for Women's Policy Research.

Hamre, B. K., & Pianta, R. C. (2004). Self-reported depression in nonfamilial caregivers: Prevalence and associations with caregiver behavior in child-care settings. *Early Childhood Research Quarterly, 19*(2), 297–318.

Hansmann, H. B. (1980). The role of nonprofit enterprise. *Yale Law School Journal, 89*, 835–901.

Hanushek, E. A. (1997). Assessing the effects of school resources on student performance: An update. *Educational Evaluation and Policy Analysis, 19*(2), 141–164.

Hanushek, E. A., Kain, J. F., & Rivkin, S. G. (2001). *Why public schools lose teachers*. Greensboro, NC: Smith Richardson Foundation.

Harms, T., Clifford, R. M., & Cryer, D. (1998). *Early childhood environment rating scale* (Rev. ed.). New York: Teachers College Press.

Harms, T., & Clifford, R. M. (1989). *The Family Day Care Rating Scale*. New York: Teachers College Press.

Harms, T., Cryer, D., & Clifford, R. M. (1990). *Infant/Toddler Environment Rating Scale*. New York: Teachers College.

Hart, K., & Schumacher, R. (2005). *Making the case: Improving Head Start teacher qualifications requires increased investment* (Head Start Series, Paper No. 1). Washington, DC: Center for Law and Social Policy.

Hatch, L. (2006). *Labor turnover in the child-care industry: Exit or voice? Preliminary findings*. University of Massachusetts, Amherst.

Helburn, S. W. (1995). *Cost, quality, and child outcomes in child care centers*. Denver: University of Colorado, Economics Department.

Helburn, S. W., & Bergmann, B. R. (2002). *America's child care problem: The way out*. New York: Palgrave.

Herzenberg, S., Price, M., & Bradley, D. (2005). *Losing ground in early childhood education: Declining workforce qualifications in an expanding industry, 1979–2004*. Washington, DC: Economic Policy Institute.

Hirsch, E. (2005). *Listening to the experts: A report on the 2004 South Carolina teacher working conditions survey*. Hillsborough, NC: Center for Teaching Quality.

Honig, A. S., & Hirallal, A. (1998). Which counts more for excellence in childcare staff: Years in service, education level, or ECE coursework? *Early Child Development and Care, 145,* 31–46.

Howes, C. (1997). Children's experiences in center-based child care as a function of teacher background and adult : child ratio. *Merrill-Palmer Quarterly, 43,* 404–425.

Howes, C., & Hamilton, C. E. (1993). The changing experience of child care: Changes in teachers and in teacher–child relationships and children's social competence with peers. *Early Childhood Research Quarterly, 8*(1), 15–32.

Howes, C., James, J., & Ritchie, S. (2003). Pathways to effective teaching. *Early Childhood Research Quarterly, 18*(1), 104–120.

Human Services Policy Center. (2003). *Family, friend, and neighbor caregivers in Washington State* (Fact Sheet). Seattle: University of Washington.

Hutchinson, B. L. (1994). The value of developmentally appropriate practice for all children. In S. G. Goffin & D. E. Day (Eds.), *New perspectives in early childhood teacher education: Bringing practitioners into the debate* (pp. 146–155). New York: Teachers College Press.

Isenberg, J. P. (2000). The state of the art in early childhood professional preparation. In D. Horm-Wingerd & M. Hyson (Eds.), *New teachers for a new century: The future of early childhood professional preparation* (pp. 15–58). Jessup, MD: U.S. Department of Education.

Johnson-Staub, C. (2005). *Infant and toddler state-level caregiver training and workforce initiatives* (Massachusetts Capacity Study Research Brief). Wellesley, MA: Wellesley College, Center for Research on Women.

Jorde Bloom, P. (1986). Teacher job satisfaction: A framework for analysis. *Early Childhood Research Quarterly, 1,* 167–183.

Jorde-Bloom, P. (1988). Closing the gap: An analysis of teachers and administrator perceptions of organizational climate in the early childhood setting. *Teachers and Teacher Education, 4*(2), 111–120.

Jorde-Bloom, P. (1996). The quality of work life in NAEYC accredited and non-accredited early childhood programs. *Early Education and Development, 7*(4), 301–317.

Jorde-Bloom, P., & Sheerer, M. (1992). The effect of leadership training on child care program quality. *Early Childhood Research Quarterly, 7*(4), 579–594.

Kagan, S. L., & Cohen, N. E. (1997). *Not by chance: Creating an early care and education system for America's children* (Full Report). New Haven, CT: Yale University, Bush Center in Child Development and Social Policy.

Kagan, S. L., & Rigby, E. (2003). *Policy matters: Improving the readiness of children for school: Recommendations for state policy.* Washington, DC: Center for the Study of Social Policy.

Kagan, S. L., Tarrant, K., & Berliner, A. (2005). *Building a professional development system in South Carolina: Review and analysis of other states' experiences.* New York: Columbia University, National Center for Children and Families.

Katz, L. (2003). *The state of the art of early childhood education.* Paper based on a lecture presented at the University of Louisiana, Lafayette.

Keller, B. (2006). NCATE accredits its first online teacher-training program. *Education Week, 26*(11), 12.

Kennedy, M. (1997). The connection between research and practice. *Educational Researcher, 26*(7), 4–12.

Kontos, S., Howes, C., & Galinsky, E. (1996). Does training make a difference to quality in family child care? *Early Childhood Research Quarterly, 11*(4), 427–445.

Kontos, S., Howes, C., Galinsky, E., & Shinn, M. (1995). *Quality in family child care and relative care.* New York: Families and Work Institute.

Kontos, S., & Stremmel, A. J. (1988). Caregivers' perceptions of working conditions in a child care environment. *Early Childhood Research Quarterly, 3*(1), 77–90.

Kramer, J. F. (1994). Defining competences as readiness to learn. In S. G. Goffin & D. E. Day (Eds.), *New perspectives in early childhood teacher education: Bringing practitioners into the debate* (pp. 29–36). New York: Teachers College Press.

LaFrance, S., Barengo, S., Parsons, G., Friel, C., Latham, N., & Lanzerotti, R. (2004). *Building the field that builds the future: A comprehensive evaluation of San Francisco CARES and WAGES Plus: Executive summary.* San Francisco: LaFrance Associates, LLC.

Lambert, R. G., O'Donnell, M., Abbott-Shim, M., & Kusherman, J. (2006, April). *The effect of the Creative Curriculum training and technical assistance on Head Start classroom quality.* Paper presented at the annual meeting of the American Educational Research Association.

Laurence, W., Hass, B., Burr, E., Fuller, B., Gardner, M., Hayward, G., et al. (2002). *Incentives for attracting and retaining K–12 teachers: Lessons for early education* (Policy Brief 02-3). Berkeley: University of California, Policy Analysis for California Education.

Layzer, J. I., & Goodson, B. D. (2006). *National study of child care for low-income families. Care in the home: A description of family child care and the experiences of the families and children who use it. Wave 1 report.* Cambridge, MA: Abt Associates, Inc.

Legal Momentum. (2006). *The family initiative legislation.* Retrieved February 13, 2006, from http://www.legalmomentum.org/fi/leg/

LeMoine, S., & Azer, S. L. (2006a). *Center child care licensing requirements (October 2006): Minimum early childhood education (ECE) preservice qualifications and annual ongoing training hours for teachers and master teachers.* Retrieved, May 7, 2007, from http://www.nccic.org/pubs/cclicensingreq/cclr-teachers.html

LeMoine, S., & Azer, S. L. (2006b). *Child care licensing requirements (April 2006): Minimum early childhood education (ECE) preservice qualifications, orientation/initial licensure, and annual ongoing training hours for family child care providers.* Retrieved July 17, 2006, from http://www.nccic.org/pubs/cclicensingreq/cclr-famcare.html

LeMoine, S., & Azer, S. L. (2006c). *Child care licensing requirements (November 2005): Minimum early childhood education (ECE) preservice qualifications, administrative, and annual ongoing training hours for directors*. Retrieved July 17, 2006, from http://www.nccic.org/pubs/cclicensingreq/cclr-directors .html

Levin, H. M., & McEwan, P. J. (2001). *Cost-effectiveness analysis: Methods and applications* (2nd ed.). Thousand Oaks, CA: Sage.

Light, P. C. (2003). *The health of the human services workforce*. New York: Center for Public Service, Brookings Institution and Wagner School of Public Service, New York University.

Living Wage Resource Center. (2005). *Living wage successes*. Brooklyn, NY: Author.

Lobman, C., Ryan, S., & McLaughlin, J. (2005). Reconstructing teacher education to prepare qualified preschool teachers: Lessons from New Jersey [Electronic version]. *Early Childhood Research & Practice, 7*. Retrieved November 10, 2006, from http://ecrp.uiuc.edu/v7n2/lobman.html

LoCasale-Crouch, J., Konold, T., Pianta, R. C., Howes, C., Burchinal, M., Bryant, D., et al. (2007). Observed classroom quality profiles in state-funded pre-kindergarten programs and associations with teacher, program, and classroom characteristics. *Early Childhood Research Quarterly, 22*(1), 3–17.

Lortie, D. C. (1975). *Schoolteacher: A sociological study*. Chicago: University of Chicago Press.

Love, J. M., Schochet, P. Z., & Meckstroth, A. L. (1996). *Are they in any real danger? What research does—and doesn't—tell us about child care quality and children's well-being*. Princeton, NJ: Mathematica Policy Research.

Lowenstein, A., Ochshorn, S., Kagan, S. L., & Fuller, B. (2004). *The effects of professional development efforts and compensation on quality of early care and education services*. Denver, CO: National Conference of State Legislatures.

Magnuson, K. A. (2002). *The intergenerational benefits of maternal education: The effect of increases in mothers' educational attainment on children's academic outcomes*. Northwestern University, Evanston, IL.

Maine Department of Health and Human Services Office of Child Care and Head Start. (2005). *Child care tax credits*. Retrieved March 1, 2006, from http://www.maine.gov/dhhs/occhs/taxcredits.htm

Marshall, N. L., Dennehy, J., Johnson-Staub, C., & Robeson, W. W. (2005). *Characteristics of the current early education and care workforce serving 3–5 year-olds* (Massachusetts Capacity Study Research Brief). Wellesley, MA: Wellesley College, Center for Research on Women.

Martinez-Beck, I., & Zaslow, M. (2006). Introduction: The context for critical issues in early childhood professional development. In M. Zaslow & I. Martinez-Beck (Eds.), *Critical issues in early childhood professional development* (pp. 1–16). Baltimore: Paul H. Brookes.

Maryland State Department of Education. (2005). *Division of Early Childhood Office of Child Care, Credentialing Branch: Training vouchers and reimbursement*. Retrieved February 28, 2006, from http://www.dhr.state.md.us/cca/creden/mdcred.htm

Maxwell, K. L., Feild, C. C., & Clifford, R. M. (2006). Defining and measuring professional development in early childhood research. In M. Zaslow & I. Martinez-Beck (Eds.), *Critical issues in early childhood professional development* (pp. 21–48). Baltimore: Paul H. Brookes.

Maxwell, K. L., Lim, C.-I., & Early, D. M. (2006). *Early childhood teacher preparation programs in the United States: National report.* Chapel Hill: University of North Carolina, Frank Porter Graham Child Development Institute.

McCormick Tribune Center for Early Childhood Leadership. (2005). *Program administration scale: Measuring early childhood leadership and management.* Retrieved February 27, 2006, from http://cecl.nl.edu/technical/pasoverview.htm

McMullen, M. B. (2003, April). *Acquiring and supporting developmentally appropriate beliefs and practices in early care and education professionals.* Paper presented at the biennial meeting of the Society for Research in Child Development, Tampa, FL.

McMullen, M. B., & Alat, K. (2002). Education matters in the nurturing of beliefs of preschool caregivers and teachers [Electronic version]. *Early Childhood Research and Practice, 4.* Retrieved January 22, 2007, from http://ecrp.uiuc.edu/v4n2/mcmullen.html

Minnesota Department of Human Services. (2005). *School readiness in child care settings: A developmental assessment of children in 22 accredited child care centers.* St. Paul: Author.

Minnesota Licensed Family Child Care Association. (2006). *MLFCCA mentor page.* Retrieved February 2, 2006, from http://www.mlfcca.org/MENTORB.htm

Mitchell, A. (2005). *Stair steps to quality: A guide for states and communities developing quality rating systems for early care and education.* Alexandria, VA: United Way of America, Success by 6.

Mitchell, A., & LeMoine, S. (2005). *Cross-sector early childhood professional development: A technical assistance paper.* Washington, DC: National Child Care Information Center.

Mitchell, A., & Morgan, G. (2000). *New perspectives on compensation strategies.* Boston: Center for Career Development in Early Care and Education at Wheelock College.

Mitchell, A., & Stoney, L. (2004). *Financing early childhood care and education systems: A standards-based approach*: Alliance for Early Childhood Finance.

Mitchell, A., Stoney, L., & Dichter, H. (2001). *Financing child care in the United States: An expanded catalog of current strategies, 2001 edition.* Kansas City, MO: Ewing Marion Kauffman Foundation.

Montilla, M. D., Twombly, E. C., & De Vita, C. J. (2001). *Models for increasing child care worker compensation.* Washington, DC: Urban Institute.

Moon, J., & Burbank, J. (2004). *The early childhood education career and wage ladder: A model for improving quality in early learning and care programs.* Seattle, WA: Economic Opportunity Institute.

Morgan, K. J. (2005). The "production" of child care: How labor markets shape social policy and vice versa. *Social Politics, 12*(2), 243–263.

Moses, A. R. (2006, December 1). Grading thy neighbor. *Teacher Magazine, 18,* 8.

Muijs, D., Aubrey, C., Harris, A., & Briggs, M. (2004). How do they manage? A review of the research on leadership in early childhood. *Journal of Early Childhood Research, 2*(2), 157–169.

National Association for Family Child Care. (2006). *Best practices for family child* care: Union organizing—A position statement of the National Association for Family Child Care. Salt Lake City, UT: Author.

National Association for the Education of Young Children. (1996). Developmentally appropriate practice in early childhood programs serving children from birth through age 8. Washington, DC: Author.

National Association for the Education of Young Children. (2001). NAEYC standards for early childhood professional preparation: Initial licensure programs. Retrieved May 4, 2007, from http://www.naeyc.org/faculty/pdf/2001.pdf

National Association for the Education of Young Children. (2006a, August 14). Early childhood associate degree accreditation: Congratulations to the first early childhood associate degree programs to earn NAEYC accreditation. Retrieved January 12, 2007, from http://www.naeyc.org/faculty/asdeg.asp

National Association for the Education of Young Children. (2006b). State policies on accreditation and quality rating systems and tiered reimbursement programs. Retrieved February 20, 2006, from https://www.naeyc.org/ece/critical/chart1.asp

National Association for the Education of Young Children. (n.d.). About NAEYC. Retrieved December 7, 2006, from http://www.naeyc.org/about/

National Child Care Information Center. (2004). State articulation in early childhood education. Retrieved June 12, 2006, from http://www.nccic.org/poptopics/statearticulation.html

National Child Care Information Center. (2006a). Financial incentives in quality rating systems. Retrieved May 4, 2007, from http://nccic.org/poptopics/qrs-fi.pdf

National Child Care Information Center. (2006b). State professional development systems and initiatives for the early childhood workforce. Retrieved February 2, 2006, from http://nccic.org/pubs/goodstart/state-ece.html

National Child Care Information Center. (2007). Quality rating systems: Definition and statewide systems. Retrieved May 7, 2007, from http://nccic.org/pubs/qrs-defsystems.html

National Council for Accreditation of Teacher Education. (2007, January 10). Nationally recognized programs: List of recognized programs per accredited institutions for: Early childhood education (NAEYC). Retrieved January 12, 2007, from http://www.ncate.org/public/recogPgmSPA.asp

National Early Childhood Technical Assistance Center. (n.d.). State work planning technical assistance service. Retrieved July 12, 2006, from http://www.ectac.org/default.asp

National Education Goals Panel. (1994). The national education goals report: Building a nation of learners. Washington, DC: Author.

National Infant & Toddler Child Care Initiative. (2004). State efforts that support infant & toddler caregiver education and training. Retrieved June 5, 2006, from http://www.nccic.org/itcc/publications/caregiver.htm

National Infant & Toddler Child Care Initiative. (2006). Infant/toddler child care credentials. Retrieved December 28, 2006, from http://www.nccic.org/itcc/publications/it_credentials.htm

National Institute for Child Health and Human Development Early Child Care Research Network. (1996). Characteristics of infant child care: Factors contributing to positive caregiving. *Early Childhood Research Quarterly, 11*(3), 269–306.

National Institute for Early Education Research. (2003). *Fast facts: Costs of providing quality preschool to America's 3- and 4-year-olds.* Retrieved June 15, 2006, from http://nieer.org/resources/facts/index.php?FastFactID=5

Nelson, M. K. (1990a). *Negotiated care: The experience of family day care providers.* Philadelphia: Temple University Press.

Nelson, M. K. (1990b). A study of turnover among family day care providers. *Children Today, 19*(2), 8–12, 30.

New Commission on the Skills of the American Workforce. (2007). *Tough choices or tough times.* Washington, DC: National Center on Education and the Economy.

Norris, D. J. (2001). Quality of care offered by providers with differential patterns of workshop participation. *Child and Youth Care Forum, 30*(2), 111–121.

Office of Child Development. (2006). *Reaching for the stars: A world of possibilities: Office of Child Development 2005–2006 annual report.* Harrisburg, PA: Author.

Office of Head Start. (2004). Innovations in meeting the needs of Head Start teachers at the University of Texas at San Antonio [Electronic version]. *Communique: Head Start Higher Education Partnerships, 3*(1). Retrieved June 25, 2006, from http://www.acf.hhs.gov/programs/hsb/publications/communiqueFEB04.htm#hbcu

Ohio, Arkansas, Illinois adopt NLU early childhood leadership quality rating tools [Electronic version]. (2007). *NCE Alumni Link-Up.* Retrieved January 22, 2007, from http://www.nl.edu/Alumni/nce-alumni-link-up-jan.cfm

Ounce of Prevention Fund. (2005). Bilingual/bicultural workgroup moves ahead [Electronic version]. *Early Edition.* Retrieved March 2, 2006, from http://www.ounceofprevention.org/early_edition/index.php?id=23

Palsha, S., & Wesley, P. W. (1998). Improving quality in early childhood environments through on-site consultation. *Topics in Early Childhood Special Education, 18*(4), 243–325.

Park-Jadotte, J., Golin, S. C., & Gault, B. (2002). *Building a stronger child care workforce: A review of studies of the effectiveness of public compensation initiatives.* Washington, DC: Institute for Women's Policy Research.

PATCH. (2004). *Resources for providers: Early childhood scholarships.* Retrieved June 20, 2006, from http://www.patchhawaii.org/Providers/scholarships.asp

Peters, H. E., & Bristow, B. (2006). Early childhood professional development programs: Accounting for spillover effects and market interventions. In M. Zaslow & I. Martinez-Beck (Eds.), *Critical issues in early childhood professional development* (pp. 339–350). Baltimore: Paul H. Brookes.

Phillips, D., Crowell, N., Whitebook, M., & Bellm, D. (2003). *English literacy levels of the early care and education workforce: A profile and associations with quality of care.* Berkeley: University of California, Center for the Study of Child Care Employment.

Phillips, D., Mekos, D., Scarr, S., McCartney, K., & Abbott-Shim, M. (2001). Within and beyond the classroom door: Assessing quality in child care centers. *Early Childhood Research Quarterly, 15*(4), 475–496.

Pianta, R. C. (2006). Standardized observation and professional development: A focus on individualized implementation and practices. In M. Zaslow & I. Martinez-Beck (Eds.), *Critical issues in early childhood professional development* (pp. 231–254). Baltimore: Paul H. Brookes.

Pianta, R. C. (2007). Preschool is school, sometimes. *Education Next, 1,* 44–49.

Pittard, M., Zaslow, M., Lavelle, B., & Porter, T. (2006). *Investing in quality: A survey of state child care and development fund initiatives.* Washington, DC: National Association of State Child Care Administrators and Child Trends with Bank Street College of Education.

Pomper, K., Blank, H., Campbell, N. D., & Schulman, K. (2005). *Be all that we can be: Lessons from the military for improving our nation's child care system: 2004 follow-up.* Washington, DC: National Women's Law Center.

Porter, T., & Kearns, S. M. (2005). *Supporting family, friend and neighbor caregivers: Findings from a survey of state policies.* New York: Bank Street College of Education, Institute for a Child Care Continuum.

Provasnik, S., & Dorfman, S. (2005). *Mobility in the teacher workforce: Findings from the condition of education, 2005.* Washington, DC: U.S. Department of Education, National Center for Education Statistics.

Qualistar. (2004). *Qualistar rating: Quality early learning.* Retrieved February 17, 2006, from http://www.qualistar.org/page.html?id=12&clear_inputs=1

Raikes, H., Wilcox, B., Peterson, C., Hegland, S., Atwater, J., Summers, J., et al. (2003). *Child care quality and workforce characteristics in four midwestern states.* Omaha, NE: Gallup Organization and Center on Children, Families, and the Law.

Raver, C. C. (2003). Does work pay psychologically as well as economically? The role of employment in predicting depressive symptoms and parenting among low-income families. *Child Development, 74*(6), 1720–1736.

Ray, A., Bowman, B., & Robbins, J. (2006). *Preparing early childhood teachers to successfully educate all children: The contribution of four-year undergraduate teacher preparation programs.* New York: Foundation for Child Development.

Rhode Island Department of Human Services. (2005). *Child Care Provider Rite Care (CCPRC) for CCAP approved family child-care providers.* Retrieved April 26, 2007, from http://www.dhs.ri.gov/dhs/heacre/drchiccf.htm

Richmond, J. B., & Kotelchuck, M. (1984). Commentary on changed lives. In J. R. Berrueta-Clement, L. J. Schweinhart, W. S. Barnett, A. S. Epstein, & D. P. Weikart, *Changed lives: The effects of the Perry Preschool Program on youths through age 19* (pp. 204–210). Ypsilanti, MI: High/Scope Educational Research Foundation.

Rowe, D. J., Early, B., & Loubier, D. (1994). Facilitating the distinctive role of infant and toddler teachers. In S. G. Goffin & D. E. Day (Eds.), *New perspectives in early childhood teacher education: Bringing practitioners into the debate* (pp. 17–28). New York: Teachers College Press.

Ruopp, R., Travers, J., Glantz, F., & Coelen, C. (1979). *Children at the center: Final report of the National Day Care Study.* Cambridge, MA: Abt Associates.

Russell, S., & Rogers, J. (2005). T.E.A.C.H. Early Childhood®: Providing strategies and solutions for the early childhood workforce. *Child Care Exchange*, March/April, 69–73.

Ryan, S., & Ackerman, D. J. (2005). Using pressure and support to create a qualified workforce [Electronic version]. *Education Policy Analysis Archives, 13*. Retrieved January 19, 2007, from http://epaa.asu.edu/epaa/v13n23/

Ryan, S., Hornbeck, A., & Frede, E. (2004). Mentoring for change: A time use study of teacher consultants in preschool reform [Electronic version]. *Early Childhood Research and Practice, 6*. Retrieved January 19, 2007, from http://ecrp.uiuc.edu/v6n1/ryan.html

Salamon, L. M. (Ed.). (2002). *The tools of government: A guide to the new governance.* New York: Oxford University Press.

Saluja, G., Early, D. M., & Clifford, R. M. (2002). Demographic characteristics of early childhood teachers and structural elements of early care and education in the United States [Electronic version]. *Early Childhood Research and Practice, 4*. Retrieved January 19, 2007, from http://ecrp.uiuc.edu/v7n2/lobman.html

Schumacher, R., Ewen, D., Hart, K., & Lombardi, J. (2005). *All together now: State experiences in using community-based child care to provide pre-kindergarten.* Washington, DC: Center for Law and Social Policy.

Schweinhart, L. J., Barnes, H. V., & Weikert, D. P. (1993). *Significant benefits: The High/Scope Perry Preschool study through age 27.* Ypsilanti, MI: High/Scope Press.

Scott-Little, C., Kagan, S. L., & Frelow, V. S. (2005). *Inside the content: The breadth and depth of early learning standards.* Greensboro, NC: SERVE.

Seavey, D. (2004). *The cost of frontline turnover in long-term care* (Practice & Policy Report). Washington, DC: Better Jobs Better Care.

Service Employees International Union. (2005). *SEIU child care providers uniting to put kids first.* Retrieved December 5, 2006, from http://www.kidsfirstseiu .org/index.asp?Type=B_BASIC&SEC=%7B1862BF8E-E432-4048-994E-582B315C786D%7D

Shkodriani, G. (2004). *Seamless pipeline from two-year to four-year institutions for teacher training: Preparing tomorrow's teachers to use technology policy brief.* Denver, CO: Community College Center for Policy, Education Commission of the States.

Smith, L. K., Sarkar, M., Perry-Manning, S., & Schmalzried, B. (2006). *NACCRRA's national survey of child care resource & referral training: Building a training system for the child care workforce.* Arlington, VA: National Association of Child Care Resource & Referral Agencies.

South Dakota Department of Social Services. (2006). *Building blocks child care mentor program.* Retrieved February 2, 2006, from http://www.state.sd.us/social/CCS/MentorProgram/MentorHome.htm

Stayton, V. D., & McCollum, J. (2002). Unifying general and special education: What does the research tell us? *Teacher Education and Special Education, 25*(3), 211–218.

Stoney, L. (2004a). *Collective management of early childhood programs: Approaches that aim to maximize efficiency, help improve quality and stabilize the industry.* Ithaca,

NY: Cornell University and the National Smart Start Technical Assistance Center.

Stoney, L. (2004b). *Financing quality rating systems: Lessons learned.* United Way of American, Success by 6.

Stremmel, A. J., Benson, M. J., & Powell, D. R. (1993). Communication, satisfaction, and emotional exhaustion among child care center staff: Directors, teachers, and assistant teachers. *Early Childhood Research Quarterly, 8*(2), 221–233.

Talan, T. N., & Bloom, P. J. (2005). *Program administration scale.* New York: Teachers College Press.

Tennessee Family Child Care Alliance. (2006). *Project T.O.P.S.T.A.R (Tennessee's Outstanding Providers Supported Through Available Resources).* Retrieved April 5, 2006, from http://www.tfcca.homestead.com/topstar.html

Toledo Public Schools and Toledo Federation of Teachers. (2002). *Intern intervention evaluation: A professional development plan for classroom performance.* Toledo, OH: Author.

Tout, K., & Zaslow, M. (2004). *Tiered reimbursement in Minnesota child care settings: A report of the Minnesota child care policy research partnership.* Washington, DC: Child Trends.

Tout, K., Zaslow, M., & Berry, D. (2006). Quality and qualifications: Links between professional development and quality in early care and education settings. In M. Zaslow & I. Martinez-Beck (Eds.), *Critical issues in early childhood professional development* (pp. 77–110). Baltimore: Paul H. Brookes.

Twombly, E. C., Montilla, M., & De Vita, C. J. (2001). *State initiatives to increase compensation for child care workers.* Washington, DC: Urban Institute, Center on Nonprofits and Philanthropy.

UNESCO. (2006). *Education for all global monitoring report 2007: Strong foundations: Early childhood care and education.* Paris: Author.

U.S. Department of Education. (2004, November 22). *No Child Left Behind: A desktop reference: Early childhood professional development* (II-A-5-2151 (E)). Retrieved January 12, 2007, from http://www.ed.gov/admins/lead/account/nclbreference/page_pg20.html#ii-a5–2151e

U.S. Department of Education. (n.d.). *The Office of Special Education Programs.* Retrieved July 2, 2006, from http://www.ed.gov/about/offices/list/osers/osep/index.html

U.S. Department of Labor Employment and Training Administration. (2005). *Quality child care initiative: 1999–2004.* Washington, DC: Author.

Walker, J. R. (1995). Public policy and the supply of child care services. In D. Blau (Ed.), *The economics of child care* (pp. 51–77). New York: Russell Sage Foundation.

Walsh, M., Graham, M., & Baker, K. (2004). *Building the capacity for degreed teachers for Florida's pre-kindergarten system.* Tallahasee, FL: Florida TaxWatch Center for Educational Performance and Accountability with the FSU Center for Prevention & Early Intervention Policy.

Wannan, L. (2005, October 20). *A cautionary tale from Australia: Briefing session notes.* Paper presented at the Canadian Council on Social Development, Ottawa.

Warner, M., Adriance, S., Barai, N., Hallas, J., Markeson, B., Morrisey, T., et al. (2004). *Economic development strategies to promote quality child care.* Ithaca, NY: Linking Economic Development and Child Care Research Project.

Washington State Child Care Resource and Referral Network. (2006). *Building blocks.* Retrieved February 2, 2006, from http://www.childcarenet.org/ Building%20Blocks.htm

Weaver, R. H. (2002a). Predictors of quality and commitment in family child care: Provider education, personal resources, and support. *Early Education and Development, 13*(3), 265–282.

Weaver, R. H. (2002b). The roots of quality care: Strengths of master providers. *Young Children, 57*(1), 16–22.

Weber, R. B. (2005). *Measurement of child care arrangement stability: A review and case study using Oregon child care subsidy data.* Unpublished dissertation, Oregon State University, Corvallis, OR.

Welch-Ross, M., Wolf, A., Moorehouse, M., & Rathgeb, C. (2006). Improving connections between professional development research and early childhood policies. In M. Zaslow & I. Martinez-Beck (Eds.), *Critical issues in early childhood professional development* (pp. 369–394). Baltimore: Paul H. Brookes.

Wesley, P. W. (1994). Providing on-site consultation to promote quality in integrated child care programs. *Journal of Early Intervention, 18*(4), 391–402.

WestEd Center for Child and Family Studies. (2003). *Impact of PITC training on quality of infant/toddler care: Evaluation report.* San Francisco: Author.

WestEd Center for Child and Family Studies. (2006). *Program for Infant/Toddler Care (PITC) Partners for Quality in Fresno County, 2003–06: Evaluation report.* San Francisco: Author.

Whitebook, M. (2003). *Early education quality: Higher teacher qualifications for better learning environments—A review of the literature.* Berkeley: University of California, Center for the Study of Child Care Employment.

Whitebook, M., & Bellm, D. (1999). *Taking on turnover: An action guide for child care center teachers and directors.* Berkeley: University of California, Center for the Study of Child Care Employment.

Whitebook, M., & Bellm, D. (2004). *Lessons from CARES and other early care and education workforce initiatives in California, 1999–2004: A review of evaluations completed by Fall 2004.* Berkeley: University of California, Center for the Study of Child Care Employment.

Whitebook, M., Bellm, D., Lee, Y., & Sakai, L. (2005). *Time to revamp and expand: Early childhood teacher preparation programs in California's institutions of higher education.* Berkeley, CA: Center for the Study of Child Care Employment.

Whitebook, M., Burton, A., Montgomery, D., Hikido, C., & Chambers, J. (1996). *California child care and development compensation study: Towards promising policy and practice.* Palo Alto, CA: American Institute for Research and National Center for the Early Childhood Work Force.

Whitebook, M., Howes, C., & Phillips, D. (1990). *Who cares? Child care teachers and the quality of care in America. The national child care staffing study.* Washington, DC: Child Care Employee Project.

Whitebook, M., Howes, C., & Phillips, D. (1998). *Worthy work, unlivable wages: The national child care staffing study, 1988–1997.* Washington, DC: Center for the Child Care Workforce.

Whitebook, M., Phillips, D., Bellm, D., Crowell, N., Almaraz, M., & Jo, J. Y. (2004). *Two years in early care and education: A community portrait of quality and workforce stability, Alameda County, California.* Berkeley: University of California, Center for the Study of Child Care Employment.

Whitebook, M., Phillips, D., & Howes, C. (1993). *National child care staffing study revisited: Four years in the life of center-based care.* Oakland, CA: Child Care Employee Project.

Whitebook, M., & Sakai, L. (2003). Turnover begets turnover: An examination of job and occupational stability among child care center staff. *Early Childhood Research Quarterly, 18*(3), 273–293.

Whitebook, M., Sakai, L., Gerber, E., & Howes, C. (2001). *Then and now: Changes in child care staffing, 1994–2000.* Washington, DC: Center for the Child Care Workforce.

Whitebook, M., Sakai, L., & Howes, C. (1997). *NAEYC accreditation as a strategy for improving child care quality: An assessment by the National Center for the Early Childhood Work Force.* Washington, DC: Center for the Child Care Workforce.

Wien, C. A. (1995). *Developmentally appropriate practice in "real life": Stories of teacher practical knowledge.* New York: Teachers College Press.

Workgroup on Defining and Measuring Early Childhood Professional Development. (2005, December). *Defining and measuring early childhood professional development: Update and request for input.* PowerPoint presented at the Annual Conference of the National Association for the Education of Young Children, Washington, D.C.

Yonemura, M. V. (1994). Accomplishing my work as a teacher educator: Hopes, practices, supports, and constraints. In S. G. Goffin & D. E. Day (Eds.), *New perspectives in early childhood teacher education: Bringing practitioners into the debate* (pp. 167–181). New York: Teachers College Press.

Zellman, G. L., & Gates, S. M. (2002). *Examining the cost of military child care.* Santa Monica, CA: RAND Research.

About the Authors

Sharon Lynn Kagan is the Virginia and Leonard Marx Professor of Early Childhood and Family Policy, Co-Director of the National Center for Children and Families, and Associate Dean for Policy at Teachers College, Columbia University, and Professor Adjunct at Yale University's Child Study Center. A scholar-advocate, she has used research to help influence educational and early childhood practice and policies in the United States and in countries throughout the world. Author of over 250 articles and 13 books and recipient of hundreds of grants, her research focuses on the institutions that impact child and family life, with particular emphasis on young children and families in poverty. Augmenting her scholarship, she consults with numerous international, federal, and state ministries and agencies, the White House, Congress, governors, legislatures, and UNICEF. A former president of the National Association for the Education of Young Children and of Family Support America, she has chaired or is chairing numerous national commissions and panels, among them the U.S. National Education Goals Panel on School Readiness and the National Task Force on Standards and Accountability. She is the only woman in the history of American education to receive its three most prestigious awards: the 2004 Distinguished Service Award from the Council of Chief State School Officers (CCSSO), the 2005 James Bryant Conant Award for Lifetime Service to Education from the Education Commission of the States (ECS), and the Harold W. McGraw, Jr., Prize in Education.

Kristie Kauerz is the Early Childhood/P-3 Policy Director for Colorado Lieutenant Governor Barbara O'Brien. She also is a fourth-year doctoral student at Teachers College, Columbia University, pursuing a degree in early childhood education policy. Her research interests include reforming public education for children birth through 3rd grade (P–3 education) and the unique role of kindergarten as a link between early learning and early elementary school. She has extensive experience working with state-level policymakers on early childhood issues. She spent 5 years as program director of early learning at Education Commission of the States (ECS). Prior to that, she directed public policy analysis at the Center for Human Investment Policy at the University of Colorado–Denver, where she was the co-principal investigator on the statewide evaluations of Colorado's Consolidated Child Care Pilot Program and Colorado's Expanding Quality Infant/Toddler Care Initiative. She also worked in Colorado Governor Roy Romer's office as director of community development for families and children. She has been named an "emerging leader" in early care and education by the Children's Defense Fund. She earned her B.A. in political science from Colorado College and her M.A. in international development from the American University.

KATE TARRANT is a second-year doctoral student in curriculum and teaching, concentrating on early childhood policy. As a graduate research fellow at the National Center for Children and Families, she works on the Early Care and Education Workforce Initiative and Policy Matters. Her research interests include the application of early care and education policy to caregivers and teachers across different types of early learning settings. She is also interested in the development of comprehensive and inclusive early childhood systems. She earned her Masters Degree in Public Administration at Columbia University's School of International and Public Affairs, with a concentration in social policy. She has served as a consultant for New York City's Administration for Children Services Division of Child Care and Head Start. She previously worked as the Public Policy Specialist for Good Beginnings Alliance–Hawaii, an early childhood intermediary organization.

Index